Golda

A PLAY IN TWO ACTS

By William Gibson

SAMUEL FRENCH, INC.

25 WEST 45TH STREET   NEW YORK 10036
7623 SUNSET BOULEVARD   HOLLYWOOD 90046
LONDON   TORONTO

THE MOROSCO THEATRE

Operated by The Regency Organization, Ltd.
Lester Osterman — Stephen R. Friedman — Irwin Meyer

THE THEATRE GUILD

presents

ANNE BANCROFT

as

GOLDA

a partial portrait

by

WILLIAM GIBSON

Directed by

ARTHUR PENN

with

VIVIAN NATHAN	GERALD HIKEN	BEN HAMMER
FRANCES CHANEY	JAMES TOLKAN	SAM GRAY
ERNEST GRAVES	ZACK MATALON	SAM SCHACHT
HARRY DAVIS	NICK LA PADULA	RICHARD KUSS

Scenery & Costumes by
SANTO LOQUASTO

Lighting & Projections by
JULES FISHER

Visuals by
LUCIE D. GROSVENOR

General Manager
VICTOR SAMROCK

Produced by
PHILIP LANGNER

ERMINA MARSHALL   MARILYN LANGER

The Producers and Theatre Management are Members
of The League of New York Theatres and Producers, Inc.

CAST

1ST WITNESS	*(also Abdullah, Ben-Gurion, TV interviewer, Religious Minister, DP)*
GOLDA	
1ST ACTOR	*(also Morris, 5th Witness, DP)*
2ND ACTOR	*(also TV assistant, 6th Witness, DP)*
3RD ACTOR	*(also Arab, father, 4th Witness, British commandant, DP, cabinet minister)*
4TH ACTOR	*(also bodyguard, chairman, DP, 7th Witness, cabinet minister)*
5TH ACTOR	*(also 2nd Witness, Arab, Menachem, DP, cabinet minister)*
LOU	*(also Clara middle-aged, DP)*
SMALL GIRL	*(also Sarile as child, DP)*
SISTER	*(also young girl, Clara teen-aged, American girl, DP)*
MOTHER	*(also 3rd Witness, Sarile middle-aged, DP)*
BOY	*(also DP)*
YOUNGER BOY	*(also DP)*

4

THE STAGING

The play must announce itself at the outset as non-representational. Ninety-nine per cent factual, it is a documentary fantasia on a moral theme, and is structured on three levels, presentational, linear, and memory.

On the presentational level the numbered actors are functionaries, not dimensional characters, who create the settings, address the audience as story-tellers, and —except for Golda—assume a succession of identities as the need arises. The second level is conventionally linear, the "present time" of the Yom Kippur War of 1973. The third is memory, a summoning up in Golda of turning-points in her past which, like the "witnesses," are related associatively to the events of that war.

The movement, lighting, and other aspects of direction must establish these levels. Whatever means the actor uses to differentiate his roles—costume bits, hair, props, whatnot—his changes should be recognizable, an integral part of the staging concept. This artifice is the stage reality, a transparency, through which the historical reality may speak.

THE SET

Up left, a platform used as Golda's office, with a step or two down, but enterable from any side.

Down right, a low platform used as a bed, table, and otherwise; it leads to a higher platform, up right.

Deep rear, a row of chairs—brought from time to time onstage—on which the company sits betweenwhiles.

Golda

ACT ONE

The company seats itself at rear, houselights still on.

The 1st WITNESS comes down, spreads a blanket on the platform down right, and addresses us.

1st WITNESS. Golda?—well, I'll tell you a fable. But true! —everything here is true, and one plot. In 1921 two dozen of us came over to Palestine with her. Young, socialists, stars in our eyes. Nine days it took us to sail from New York to Boston, with a strike— and sabotage, one sailor yells at me, Your ship'll sink in mid-ocean! And it takes us, the two-week trip to Naples, forty-four days. The crew is mixing seawater into our drinking water, and the pumps and boilers start breaking down; the captain puts one seaman in irons; then the sailors leave portholes open and the food gets ruined, and all the books her young husband Morris brought are waterlogged. Golda meanwhile is on deck studying Hebrew. Fire breaks out in two bunkers, the engine room is flooded and the ship leans sideways; the captain puts the dynamo men in irons. At the Azores we stop for repairs, they try to burn the ship. Four engineers are heard saying they'll sink it before Naples, the captain puts them in irons. And finally the captain commits suicide by throwing him- self overboard; when they find his body somebody's tied his hands together to a pipe. So?—two dozen young idealists sailing off to Utopia, and below-decks human nature doing all it can to sink the ship. The question is, did it?—that's the plot, stars in your eyes, you reach! and end up holding, what, one more match in the dark?

(*The house and stage go dark, a long moment. Sound begins, whispers, lapping of water, a tramping of many feet; a shofar is blown, and dies away; a plane streaks overhead, and is gone; distant bells toll four o'clock. A phone rings, down right, and presently a spotlight steals on;* GOLDA, *elbowing up out of the blanket—seventy-five, in a night-wrap, hair in a braid, heavy-voiced and slow— picks up the phone.*)

GOLDA. Yes, what? . . . Ah, no, no—I knew, yesterday, in my bones. . . . No, look, I'll meet as soon as Moshe and Dado talk, when? . . . Then seven. Tell the others, my— (*She hangs up, bitterly—*) —generals— (*—lights a cigarette, and gets out of bed, an aged lioness, pinning up her hair.*) —half my cabinet, generals— (*Up left four actors come—two in open shirts, Israeli style, two in army khaki—with chairs and a desk, creating* GOLDA's *office in rising daylight on the platform.*) —and not one of them could smell yesterday under his nose that today it's war?

(*Sound erupts, a vast rumbling of trucks, tanks grinding, engines revving up, a clamor of foreign voices—it breaks off, the actors motionless and listening, a tableau; they recite chorus-like, and only gradually move into realistic playing.*)

1ST ACTOR. The intelligence was shit. Yesterday—
2ND. Calmly.

3RD. (*Khaki.*) The intelligence was right, we read it wrong.

1ST. Who read it wrong?

2ND. Yesterday the United States read it wrong.

4TH. (*Khaki.*) Yesterday we gave her bad advice, all of us. If—

3RD. Yesterday I said the Russians leaving Damascus—

GOLDA. (*Heavy.*) Yesterday was yesterday, let's agree to one thing, that word we don't hear again in this office. (*Dropping the nightwrap behind, in a plain washdress she trudges to join them; they move in and out around her, bringing her papers—a woman, LOU, now among them.*) Today we'll have time for one luxury only, to be attacked, when?

3RD. Six this evening.

GOLDA. So, we have ten hours. Look, I must talk to Dinitz and Keating. (LOU *goes out;* GOLDA *presides at the desk, flanked by the* 1ST *and* 4TH *actors; the* 1ST *puts on an eyepatch.*) On the call-up, the two of you agree?

1ST. Disagree, we've brought it to you.

GOLDA. (*Ponderous.*) Thank you.

4TH. I want a full mobilization for counterattack.

1ST. I say mobilize what we need to hold the lines, that's our first job—

4TH. I want to break their bones and cross the Canal.

1ST. Counterattack can wait, Golda, Dado is too— enthusiastic. There's a political consideration too, if again the world calls us the aggressor—

GOLDA. Look, political reasons I don't need to hear, military I do.

4TH. Facts, not enthusiasm—

1ST. Mobilize for defense now—

4TH. —we know what the Syrians have, over nine hundred tanks, we have 177—

1ST. —and call up the rest tonight.

4TH. When they're across the Jordan?

GOLDA. *I* have to decide between our Minister of Defense and Chief of Staff?—

1ST. Dear Prime Minister—

GOLDA. —how does a woman decide between generals?

2ND. (*A drawler.*) It comes with the job.

GOLDA. (*Pause.*) All right, the world calling us a bad name isn't such a new burden; but Syrian tanks in our backyard? I'm sorry, Moshe—

1ST. I don't insist.

GOLDA. —the call-up must be as Dado wants.

4TH. I also want a first strike.

1ST. No.

GOLDA. Preempt.

4TH. Hit them before they hit us, minutes count—

1ST. No. I do insist—we'll be condemned everywhere, get no help from anyone—

GOLDA. (*To* 4TH.) The Americans told Dinitz a hundred times don't preempt, Eban don't preempt, me don't preempt—

4TH. I can take out the Syrian airfields and missiles by noon if you move this minute.

GOLDA. You'll guarantee a six-day war again?

4TH. I guarantee you a thousand dead soldiers if you don't.

GOLDA. Dado, I have to guarantee three million live civilians. In a week we'll need help, and from the Americans; you'll risk that?

(A 5TH *actor comes to poke his head in;* LOU *follows.*)

5TH. The Lady wants me.

GOLDA. Dinitz, come in.

4TH. It will save lives—

GOLDA. (*Rises.*) More than help from the Americans?

3RD. If they help.

GOLDA. *I* guarantee that; Dinitz will see to it. It's not here I want you, Simcha, it's ringing Kissinger's doorbell.

5TH. I know—

GOLDA. How soon can you fly back?

5TH. Yom Kippur, nothing's moving—

GOLDA. You are.

LOU. The military will fly him to Cyprus; from there— (*The desk phone rings, she answers it.*)

5TH. —but this evening, if I can—

GOLDA. It's too late.

5TH. Well, if I—

GOLDA. Now. The minute you see Kissinger, the first point—

LOU. The American ambassador.

GOLDA. (*Takes phone.*) Mrs. Meir. . . . Not so good, our neighbors are calling on us today. With Soviet tanks. . . . We hear six o'clock. . . . Look, I have one message for Washington—we can strike first, and won't. . . . Can and won't, we promise won't, it's maybe not too late if the President calls on Moscow. . . . Yes, the Russians know, they all flew home from Damascus yesterday—they supply the arms, their best friends the corpses. . . . Thank you. (*She hangs up, walks the 5TH to the threshold.*) Kissinger now, the first point is we did as they said about a first strike, the second is where are the forty-eight Phantoms.

5TH. I'll push, of course I'll push—

GOLDA. The third is resupply, Nixon promised

we'd— (*Sound explodes—artillery bombardment, the roar of tanks and planes, and the air-raid sirens of Israel begin to wail here and there, climbing to full-out; the lights change to night as the actors scatter, one setting up a mike at center;* GOLDA *comes heavily to it with a speech the* 3RD *gives her, puts on glasses, and begins to read.*) Citizens of Israel. Ordeal by battle has been forced on us again. Shortly before 2:00 P.M. today the armies of Egypt and Syria launched a series of attacks in Sinai and on the Golan Heights. The Israel Defense Forces have entered the fight—our sons. We too must make any sacrifice for our independence, our freedom, our survival— (*She breaks off, closes her eyes, covers the mike with a hand—*) —our survival— (*—as the lights change to "memory light," and* GOLDA *goes deep into herself, speaking not to us:*) Survival is maybe a synonym for Jewish. The first thing I remember is my father, Moishe the carpenter, nailing boards across a door in Kiev, to keep out a pogrom. In those days pogroms were—oh, the fashionable thing, hundreds, no town without one— (*Lights on the platform up right— dreamlike, Russia 1904—and a* SMALL GIRL *dressing a doll; her* OLDER SISTER *watches her; their* MOTHER *comes in with a plate.*) —with Jews everywhere mourning, fasting—

MOTHER. Goldie, you left your plate, now I want you to eat— (*The* SMALL GIRL *ignores it, and the* MOTHER *turns on the* SISTER.) She's fasting too?—

SMALL GIRL. I'm fasting too—

MOTHER. —a wonderful example you set her, every day in black, why are you doing this to me?

SISTER. Momma, children are dead.

GOLDA. (*To us.*) —and I'm fasting—

SMALL GIRL. —for the children they killed.

MOTHER. So if you don't eat you'll be another; take a— Gevalt, she's dressing the doll in black! (*She jumps up, horrified.*) Moishe, Moishe!— oh, this Goldie has a dybbuk in her— (*She hurries out, the* SISTER *after; the* SMALL GIRL *is left alone, in fading light, and sound steals in around her—hoofbeats, rising into shouts, windows smashing, a pogrom—then breaks off; the* SMALL GIRL *stands screaming, screaming. Lights out on her;* GOLDA *puts aside the mike, speaks to us.*)

GOLDA. I have a dybbuk, yes, over and over in me it says, Live. Live, did I make it up?—God said, I've set before you two things, life and death, therefore choose life. And the dybbuk says, Here is a dream, a new land, more life for all—more life for all— (*She turns up to her office, pauses heavily.*) —so send the young to die. It has two tongues, this dybbuk—more life, more death— (*The* 3RD *actor comes to take the speech, and* GOLDA *mounts to her office;* LOU *brings in a tray of coffee, and* GOLDA *sits to the desk.*) Lou, go home and sleep.

LOU. After you.

GOLDA. I'm sleeping here, on the couch, and for two there isn't room.

LOU. First, my dear lady, you will not sleep three winks here; and second, you cannot conduct this war properly without a fresh dress.

GOLDA. (*To herself.*) Such very young boys out there, dying—

LOU. Sanctifying the name of God.

GOLDA. —I have no way to stop it. What?

LOU. It's one way the rabbis say a Jew can sanctify the name of God, to die defending other Jews.

GOLDA. (*Pause.*) Bring me a dress, tomorrow.

(LOU *nods, leaves;* GOLDA *sits over coffee and cigarette, mulling. The* 2ND *witness comes to take the mike, he is the* 5TH *actor, costumed for a different role.*)

2ND WITNESS. Golda, yes, my story is from early in '47, before the state, when our boys were ambushed by Arabs on their way to Etzion. She'd become the head of the Agency—the only one the British didn't lock up in Latrun—and I remember she made a statement, she said Jews had been dying long enough for no cause, it was time they died for their own. We were smuggling messages into the prison with the food, and Sharett read it there—she was taking his place—and sent word out it was true but "bitter as death." Well, after the ambush Golda insisted on going not only to the hospital, but into the morgue, alone. I watched, there were eight dead boys in a row on the floor, and Golda just stood looking at them, for two minutes. If she was religious I'd say she was praying; but it was her way of saying, I am at one with you. (*He takes the mike off, left; down right the* 3RD *and* 4TH *actors spread a map on the low platform, and* GOLDA *rises to come down to them.*)

GOLDA. Don't be kind to the old, Dado, how does it look?

4TH. The Golan is not good. The main thrust is developing down here, Kudne, Rafid, Juhader, at least four hundred Syrian tanks here; the Barak Brigade is being chewed up from A6 to 10—

GOLDA. How many tanks in our Barak?

3RD. The Barak is down to twenty.

GOLDA. What?

4TH. Less.

GOLDA. It's nothing, how can it be less, where are the reserves we called up?

4TH. Just coming. The 79th is here on the Yehudia road now—

GOLDA. So it's a race.

4TH. For the Jordan. If they overrun headquarters at Nafekh there's nothing between them and us, and we'll blow the bridges.

GOLDA. Give me a cigarette. What's the airforce doing?

3RD. Bombing the Canal.

GOLDA. Look, the Canal is Africa, the Jordan is our back door; call them—

4TH. Moshe did, they'll be there with first light.

GOLDA. Another hour.

3RD. It won't be like '67, we're losing planes very fast—

GOLDA. (*Unbelieving.*) To Egyptians?

3RD. To missiles, Soviet SAM's—

4TH. We're flying into the most concentrated surface-to-air network we've—

GOLDA. They said they could take out the missiles, first thing.

3RD. They can't give close support and take out the missiles both.

4TH. I asked for a first strike.

GOLDA. (*Pause.*) See if Dinitz got to Washington yet. (*The* 3RD *picks up a phone; the* 4TH *starts out.*) Dado. I'm learning here.

4TH. I know. That's all we have as of now, Golda—

3RD. (*Hangs up.*) I'll keep you in touch with the reports coming in—

4TH. Shalom— (*The two men withdraw.*)

GOLDA. (*Heavily.*) Shalom, shalom. (*She sits alone, with eyes closed, and goes into herself; the lights*

change to memory.) Israel. Israel, born 1948; died—?
A little each day since, six thousand of us that first
summer, one in a hundred—

(*The lights find* MORRIS, *silhouetted behind her; he is
the* 1ST *actor, minus the eyepatch.*)

MORRIS. It never stopped, did it? Such a dream, the
state, an irony—

GOLDA. (*Not turning.*) Morris—

MORRIS. —that this is the one place in the world
where Jews are in danger; all your life given for a
state, Goldie, next week you'll have it, and only here
could we be wiped out.

GOLDA. Morris, enough!—so jealous of what we all
dreamed—

MORRIS. (*Mildly.*) Goldie, you dreamed of a
paradise, what went wrong? (GOLDA *sits morose, not
looking at him; he turns to leave, stops.*) Are you
happy, at last?

GOLDA. Happy I never thought of, every day something impossible to do, who had time?

MORRIS. Oh, I had time.

GOLDA. You thought make a nice home, read a book,
be happy—

MORRIS. Such a dream.

GOLDA. —you should have married my mother. I
thought make a new world—

MORRIS. Whoever it cost.

GOLDA. —what else did we think of but work for it?
Fifteen hours a day in meetings and offices, and three-
thirty in the morning one man said, Goldie, don't
come in early tomorrow, come at eight.

MORRIS. (*Suddenly.*) Which man, why did we come
to this beggarly land!

GOLDA. It's ours. (*The lights lose* MORRIS; GOLDA *sits alone, eyes closed.*) Such a dream, what went wrong? (*She stands—twenty-five years younger, moves accordingly—and speaks to us:*) All right, not a state yet, May 10th, 1948— (*The* 2ND *actor enters in a khaffiyeh—as her escort, a different role—and comes to her with a black Arab robe.*) —five days to statehood, with how many Arabs around us?—

2ND. Ninety million.

GOLDA. (*To him.*) —sworn to drive us into the sea; and at the last minute Ben-Gurion sends me begging for peace.

2ND. (*Robes her.*) I'll wear this, and trust my Arabic. You will wear this, and be mute.

GOLDA. That will be the hardest.

2ND. Who else knows?

GOLDA. Here?—you and Ben-Gurion. There, I'm not so sure.

2ND. Oh, the King will be discreet, it's worth his life too.

GOLDA. Too?

2ND. The danger is real. If we're stopped, don't show fear; no believer will touch a strange woman.

GOLDA. And if it's an infidel?

2ND. I convert him. We'll change cars several times before Naharayim, to be sure we're not followed; from there we'll be driven to a house in Amman— (*Fixing her veil, he takes the cigarette out of her mouth.*) No cigarettes, please.

GOLDA. Look, without cigarettes I can't make it.

2ND. We may not make it with. Come. (*He retires a few steps;* GOLDA *turns to us as sound rises, the Arab chant of a muezzin; behind her, actors move in silently with chairs, a rug, candles, and create a room.*)

GOLDA. —ninety million Arabs around us, five times

a day on their faces praying to Allah for peace; and the one I've been bundled into Transjordan to see, in this schmotte, is—

ABDULLAH. (*Enters at rear.*) Mrs. Myerson.

GOLDA. (*Turns.*) —King Abdullah.

ABDULLAH. You look charming, I am happy you crossed safely. Please sit. (*The Arabs disappear at* ABDULLAH'S *gesture—he is the* 1ST *Witness, a different role—and he sits;* GOLDA *sits, and unveils her face.*)

GOLDA. I can't talk through a veil.

ABDULLAH. (*Smiles.*) It is why we like woman to wear it, perhaps. We are not progressive, you Jews have been so innovative in Palestine, bringing the swamps and dunes to life; share your secrets with us.

GOLDA. It's one secret—

ABDULLAH. The easier.

GOLDA. —for two thousand years pray, Next year in Jerusalem.

ABDULLAH. Of course; only the spirit makes the world fruitful.

GOLDA. Work doesn't hurt.

ABDULLAH. You know my belief that Allah scattered the Jews throughout the West that they might bring its knowledge back to us?—since we are all the children of Shem—

GOLDA. Look, in five days it's war. And the children will murder each other. (ABDULLAH *is silent.*) You're breaking your promise to me?

ABDULLAH. (*Slowly.*) That promise I made in—

GOLDA. November.

ABDULLAH. Yes—

GOLDA. Before the UN vote to partition.

ABDULLAH. —and alone among my brothers of the Arab states I accepted the UN partition—

2ND. They're not your brothers, they're your enemies.

ABDULLAH. They are my brothers and my enemies. Their view is a different one; they see the Jews returning as Europeans, no longer Semites—

GOLDA. Their view we've heard—

ABDULLAH. —but invaders.

GOLDA. —from our brother, the head of the Arab League, "This will be a war of extermination—"

ABDULLAH. Yes.

GOLDA. "—and a momentous massacre, like the Mongol massacres."

ABDULLAH. Yes.

GOLDA. Are you joining them?—that's my question. (ABDULLAH *is silent.*) In the winter you sent me a message—

ABDULLAH. I remember it.

GOLDA. —you're a Bedouin and so a man of honor, and two, a King besides, and three, a promise to a woman you'd never break.

ABDULLAH. Such good reasons—

GOLDA. So many it worried us.

ABDULLAH. But then I was alone; now I am one of five nations. And no longer master of my own destiny.

GOLDA. (*Pause.*) So the word I'll bring back is—

ABDULLAH. Mrs. Myerson, you can avert this massacre.

GOLDA. I would love to, how?

ABDULLAH. Do not proclaim your state.

GOLDA. No, no—

ABDULLAH. The Arab world cannot now accept a Jewish state in its midst, why are you in such a hurry?

GOLDA. Two thousand years I can't call a hurry.

ABDULLAH. Wait one more. I make you a new offer,

now: I will annex Palestine, unpartitioned, and merge it with Jordan; and after one year the Jews will sit in my parliament.

GOLDA. As a minority.

ABDULLAH. Proportionally. I will treat you very well—protect you—

GOLDA. Like the Germans?—fifty years you've seen us here fighting the land—

ABDULLAH. I admire it.

GOLDA. —and Arab riots, fighting each other, fighting the British army to smuggle in our survivors, there isn't a Jew among us didn't give sweat or blood; but to sit again in somebody else's parliament?—that isn't what we dreamed.

ABDULLAH. It is a dream; I offer you a compromise that is realizable.

GOLDA. Not ten Jews would stand for such a plan.

ABDULLAH. (*Turns.*) You are an Oriental Jew?

2ND. Yes.

ABDULLAH. Reason with her. Bring me an answer by May 15th, to take to my Arab friends, and we can live in peace.

2ND. You have no Arab friends, only us.

GOLDA. I can answer now. If it's war, we'll fight some more—

ABDULLAH. It means the ruin of all you achieved in fifty years—

GOLDA. —and we'll win. (*A silence.*)

ABDULLAH. Is there anything more to be said? (*He waits; then GOLDA stands.*)

GOLDA. Only shalom.

ABDULLAH. (*Stands.*) Salaam. There is so narrow a difference in how we say peace.

GOLDA. How many Jewish bodies will you bury in it? (*She walks with the 2ND actor up left, where he helps her unrobe;* ABDULLAH *remains. Sound resumes, the muezzin's call to prayer.* ABDULLAH *goes to his palms and face, praying; actors remove the room things, and one—the* MOTHER, *but a different role— lingers on the platform up right as the* 3RD *Witness.)*

3RD WITNESS. Golda, companion of kings, well, she was Goldie Mabovitch when I went to school with her in Milwaukee, and she wanted to be a teacher. She had a very bossy mother said no, no high school, she could just keep working in the store with her; so she packed up her things, lowered them out the window one night to me, and next morning got on the train to Denver. Went to high school, lived with her sister, and in her kitchen met that whole crowd of Zionists, socialists, anarchists—and of course Morris. Long dead now. But then it turned out the sister was just as bossy as the mother, so Goldie moved out on her too; found a job doing skirt-linings, and was on her own, at sixteen. I mean, if there was ever one word for Goldie it has to be independent. *(Two actors in Arab headgear enter behind* ABDULLAH *praying.)* So when a couple of years after her meeting with King Abdullah she heard the news— *(*ABDULLAH *rises, the two Arabs fire; he reels between them to escape, they follow shooting, and he falls in the dark upstage; they run off.)* —that he was assassinated, Goldie said, "And if I'd said yes to his offer?" *(Lights out on her, and up on* GOLDA's *office—the* 1ST *actor in windbreaker and eyepatch facing her across a desk map, the* 4TH *in khaki listening.)*

1ST. The Syrians are at Nafekh now.

GOLDA. What?

1ST. Headquarters pulled out at 1:15, we're throwing in reserves piecemeal. Golda, I've never felt so anxious, if we don't understand the situation fast—

(*He twists the map for her.*) Here, the Suez—the Egyptians have two thousand tanks, we're holding the Canal with 280, we're throwing in reserves piecemeal! Forget the Bar-Lev line—it's gone—

GOLDA. You're telling me what, the whole front is collapsing?

1ST. It may be, will be if we don't shorten the line—

4TH. Pull back?

1ST. We can't save the Bar-Lev forts—

GOLDA. Pull back to where?

1ST. First, evacuate all the Bar-Lev strongholds tonight—

4TH. Abandon the Canal?

1ST. —and withdraw to a new line a dozen kilometers back—

4TH. I mean to cross it.

1ST. Golda, ask Bar-Lev himself—

4TH. I have a counterattack shaping up.

1ST. —we can't push the Egyptians back now—

4TH. Of course we can. You've lost your confidence, Moshe.

1ST. (*Shaken.*) If we try it and fail, the fate of Israel will be at stake. (*A silence.* GOLDA *lights a cigarette.*)

GOLDA. (*Stolid.*) Excuse me— (*She leaves them in dimming light over the desk map, comes down from her office, and stands trembling with palms over her eyes;* LOU *comes in with a trayful, stops.*)

LOU. You're gray.

GOLDA. I think I'm going out of my senses. Moshe says it's a catastrophe, retreat—

LOU. No—

GOLDA. (*To herself.*) The work of a lifetime? I'll kill myself first—

LOU. What?

GOLDA. If we lose this war, I'll kill myself, yes—

LOU. (*Stares.*) You're serious.

GOLDA. —what they do to each other we know, think what they'll do to our Jews—

LOU. First, I have here only soup, not poisonous enough, and second, you cannot kill yourself before the election.

GOLDA. (*Grim pause.*) Lose the election too I'll kill myself first and second. Ask Lior to find Bar-Lev. (LOU *takes the tray up to the office, and sound comes in, shells exploding, half-intelligible voices on radio crackling—*)

> —*Low on ammunition, sir, can I withdraw to re-load?*
>
> —*No. Use small arms.*
>
> —*Tiger here, they're coming from the south, two thousand yards, about 40 of them.*
>
> —*Hold fire till eight hundred.*
>
> —*Only one shell per tank, sir.*
>
> —*Give me another half hour, you'll be getting reinforcements, please hold on!*
>
> —*Sir, I can't hold on.*
>
> —*For God's sake, hold on for ten minutes, help's on the way—*

(—*until* GOLDA *half covers her ears and turns, going deep into herself; sound dies—*) Didn't I know what an old invalid was good for?— (—*into a solo cello playing Bach, the 5th Suite saraband; light changes into a green dapple of leaflight—*) —retired, five years ago in the garden— (—*and a* WOMAN *brings a chair down right;* GOLDA *sits, takes her hand—*) —with my children, Sarile— (—*and a* BOY *and* GIRL *run in, to pose around* GOLDA's *feet for a smiling photo.*) —and grandchildren. Menachem! we're ready— (*Sound stops; a* MAN *comes to take his place, cellobow in hand.*) I made one mistake in my life—

MAN. Yes, mother.

GOLDA. —I should never have left the kibbutz. But now I have my own—

WOMAN. Hold still, momma.

BOY. Grandma, why are your legs different?

GOLDA. Who says they're different?

BOY. My eyes say, one is fatter—

GOLDA. Maybe one of your eyes is fatter.

BOY. Oh?—that's what philosophers call the sub-ject-object relationship—

GOLDA. Three times a day I get an inferiority com-plex from him. Look, first I broke it, then it got phlebitis, then a lunatic threw a grenade into the old Knesset and—

WOMAN. Hold still, momma.

BOY. (*Scrambles up.*) The dog, get the dog—

GOLDA. About that dog I'm not as enthused as the dog is about me— (*But the group is slipping away as she glances, disappearing in shadows—the* WOMAN *last, letting go of* GOLDA's *hand—*)

WOMAN. Momma—momma— (—*until* GOLDA *sits alone, listening to a child's voice call like an echo.*)

SMALL GIRL. (*Off.*) Momma—momma— (*She turns in with a doll—dreamlike, clothes 1930's—not seeing* GOLDA, *but spying a* YOUNGER BOY *opposite, who throws a strapful of schoolbooks on the floor.*) Menachem—

YOUNGER BOY. She's not here, stupid, so shut up.

SMALL GIRL. My dolly's sick, I want momma—

YOUNGER BOY. Let's call her. Mother!

SMALL GIRL, YOUNGER BOY. (*Together.*) Momma! Mother! Momma!

YOUNGER BOY. (*Taunting.*) Ha ha, she's in Haifa
at a meeting.

SMALL GIRL. (*Tearful.*) Momma— (*She turns out;*
MORRIS *turns in, with a book.*)

MORRIS. What's the difficulty here?

YOUNGER BOY. There's nobody to carry my cello,
where's mother?

MORRIS. Ah, now cello lessons I approve, I'll help
carry—

YOUNGER BOY. I want *her,* here.

MORRIS. Here I'm afraid she isn't.

YOUNGER BOY. Where is she?

MORRIS. In Geneva, at a meeting. Come, I'll—

YOUNGER BOY. I want *her,* I want *her*—

MORRIS. Menachem, dear— (*The* BOY *wheels away,
the* SMALL GIRL *turns in opposite.*) Sarile?

SMALL GIRL. I didn't know you're visiting, poppa.

MORRIS. Just—waiting to see your momma—

SMALL GIRL. She's away.

MORRIS. Oh. Where?

SMALL GIRL. She's in New York at a meeting.

MORRIS. (*Depressed.*) So. So.

GOLDA. (*Eyes closed.*) Forgive me—forgive me—

MORRIS. Well, should I read some more to you?—
see, I brought for entertainment a masterpiece I think
you'll both like—

YOUNGER BOY. What's it about?

MORRIS. Ideals. Listen, he tells right away. (MORRIS
*settles cross-legged, with the book; the children come
to lie on their bellies.*) "At a certain village in La
Mancha, there lived not long ago one of those old-
fashioned gentlemen who are never without a lance on
a rack, an old target, and a skinny horse."

GOLDA. (*Not turning.*) What's wrong with ideals?

MORRIS. (*Mildly.*) What's wrong with the real world?

GOLDA. Everything; ideals are how we change it.

MORRIS. Children, here and now, that's an ideal too—

GOLDA. Morris, I want them to grow up in a world that's safe.

MORRIS. I want them to grow up with a mother, Goldie. How do you feel when they're sick and need you?

GOLDA. (*Pause.*) Guilty. Whatever I do. To them, to the cause—

(*The* 2ND *actor enters down left;* LOU *is in the office.*)

2ND. (*The drawler.*) I'm told the Lady sent for me—

LOU. She's down the hall. (GOLDA *rises heavily.*)

MORRIS. Such a stateswoman—

GOLDA. Bar-Lev, I need eyes!

MORRIS. —your hands full of everything except them—

GOLDA. Could you do me a big favor?— (*The lights lose* MORRIS *and the children.*)

2ND. I'll try.

GOLDA. —leave your work as Minister of Commerce?

2ND. The supermarkets are mobbed, Golda, I'm— calming the panic.

GOLDA. Calm mine.

(*The* 4TH *actor comes in, with memos.*)

4TH. Golda—

2ND. (*Appraises her.*) You're a rock.

4TH. —I must hold onto the Canal, our defense is counterattack.

GOLDA. (*To* 2ND.) I don't like what I hear.

4TH. Fall back to a new line and—

GOLDA. —you can't counterattack.

4TH. Not and cross the Canal.

2ND. Tell me what I can do.

GOLDA. Fly up to the Golan tonight, talk with the commanders there. Look, how soon would you counter-attack on the Suez?

4TH. (*Gives her the memos.*) How soon will you get me the replacements I lose?

GOLDA. The minute Dinitz gets to Washington.

4TH. It depends, I have to see if Bren's division—

GOLDA. So go down and see! Chaim, fly up now and tell me what *you* think. (*She walks him left.*) Also why an army retires its best generals to the super-markets—

2ND. Let's turn back the Arabs first.

GOLDA. Yes, after we win.

(*The* 2ND *leaves, left; the* 4TH *lingers, right.*)

4TH. Golda.

GOLDA. You're still here?

4TH. I salute you. (*He goes out;* LOU *remains.*)

LOU. And how much poison am I to order, my dear lady?

GOLDA. Enough for both of us.

LOU. Oh?

GOLDA. But we'll wait till tomorrow. (*She trudges up to her office, to read the memos; the lighting ex-plodes, in a flood of orange fireglare; then slowly fades—*)

LOU. Soviet missiles. (*—and* LOU *turns down left, another Witness.*) I went to Moscow with Golda in '48, when she was our first Ambassador. But how to meet the Jews of Russia after thirty years we didn't see; even relatives we were afraid to contact, for their sake, Zionism was a crime— (GOLDA *picks up her phone*—)

GOLDA. Get me Dinitz. (—*and replaces it.*)

LOU. —and in the Moscow synagogue only a handful of shabby old Jews would still come. So Golda said on Rosh Hashanah the entire legation would go, and we notified the Rabbi, and that day in the street of the synagogue we were mobbed by fifty thousand Jews, old men and women, teenagers, Red Army soldiers, mothers with babies, stretching out hands and calling in Yiddish, Goldele, Goldele, leben zolst du, Goldele, and when the cantor saw the Star of David on our military attaché's hat he *shrieked!* —and to those thousands and thousands of Jews blowing her kisses, crying, kissing her dress, Golda said one sentence, A dank eich vos ihr seit geblieben Yidden, Thank you for remaining Jews. (*Down right the 5TH actor in a topcoat sits with a phone in the chair; GOLDA's phone rings.*) A photograph of the crowd was taken by a twelve-year-old boy with a birthday camera—

GOLDA. Yes?

5TH. Mrs. Meir— Hello, hello— Operator—

LOU. —and for weeks people on the street would whisper to us, I have the picture, I have the picture—

GOLDA. (*Testy.*) No, I'll hold.

LOU. —and copies travelled everywhere. In Siberia a girl from Vilna, sentenced to work in the lumber woods, was at the fire warming her chunk of frozen bread when she saw a man spying on her among the trees; he said, Are you Jewish? and she said yes, and out of his rags he took the torn picture and whispered, There is a Jewish state—

5TH. Mrs. Meir?

GOLDA. Simcha.

5TH. I'm here. Finally, what a trip—

LOU. (*Over.*) And after thirty years the Soviets knew they still had a Jewish problem.

GOLDA. You saw Kissinger? (LOU *leaves; lights up on* GOLDA *and the* 5TH.)

5TH. At six o'clock. I just left him—

GOLDA. And the Phantoms?

5TH. He knows we didn't preempt and approves, he says it was the right decision—

GOLDA. A medal I don't need. Phantoms are enough.

5TH. I said yes but it laid a heavy responsibility on his government—

GOLDA. So when do we get them?

5TH. He has to check it out with the Pentagon. I'm to—

GOLDA. Check what, Nixon himself promised me.

5TH. It's a mess here, the police are on Agnew's doorstep, Nixon is locked up with his tapes, nobody—

GOLDA. (*Flat.*) Simcha.

5TH. Yes.

GOLDA. Get the Phantoms.

5TH. Of course, of course. I'm to call him—

GOLDA. Tell him we lost planes today like flies. Dado gives me here a new list, tanks also, spare parts, electronic things, you'll have it in the morning.

5TH. I'll do everything I—

GOLDA. Simcha, half of this war is being fought by you. Such a thought frightens you?

5TH. Yes.

GOLDA. Good. (*She hangs up; lights out on the* 5TH *actor, who moves the chair up right as he leaves; down left a* BODYGUARD—*the* 4TH *actor, a different role—brings in a chair and sits,* GOLDA *scowling at the memos.*) And in my old age I'm in the munitions business? (*She flings them down on the desk, pauses in a reach for cigarettes, heavily.*) The Jewish homeland must be a model for the redemption of the human race, who said it?— Ben-Gurion, Milwaukee, 1916. I heard him, did any of us dream of this killing? (*Her pack is empty, she slaps it on the desk, and marches to the office edge, lighter in hand.*) Is anybody down there?

BODYGUARD. Just me, Golda.

GOLDA. (*Trudges down.*) Hymie, I'm all out again.

BODYGUARD. (*Rises.*) Sure, here. (GOLDA *takes a cigarette from his pack; lights down on the office.*) Why don't you let me drive you home and get a night's sleep?

GOLDA. Who will answer the phone—

BODYGUARD. Keep them, I got more in the car. (*She lights it.*) First time I drove you, remember?—

GOLDA. No.

BODYGUARD. —to be sworn in? you sat in the front seat, I said, Mrs. Meir, please sit in the back seat, you're the Prime Minister now, you said, I didn't do anything yet.— Things have changed.

GOLDA. Yes.

BODYGUARD. I'll check outside.

GOLDA. Yes— (*He goes out;* GOLDA *sits heavily in the chair, eyes closed, going into herself; the lights change to memory.*) —things have changed. 1917, 18—rid of the Kaiser and Czar, no more tyrants, peace and socialism— Oh, like a young girl this century was, such a beauty— (MORRIS *in 1915 garb stands in the shadows behind the chair up right.*) —and so much evil in her, Stalin, the depression, Hitler, World War II, the Holocaust, the atom bomb—

MORRIS. Where did it come from—

GOLDA. It looked so easy, sweep out the leftovers—

MORRIS. —the evil?

GOLDA. —build a new land with young people, hard workers, happy—

MORRIS. You did think be happy once. 1915—

GOLDA. (*Not turning.*) For everybody, yes.

MORRIS. —in Milwaukee again, you wrote a postcard to—

GOLDA. No.

MORRIS. —yes, I remember on the back—

GOLDA. No.

MORRIS. "You'll never guess who arrived last night— Morris—"

GOLDA. No.

MORRIS. "—I'm the happiest person alive."

GOLDA. (*Eyes closed.*) Yes.

MORRIS. And I said, Goldie— (*He comes around the chair up right to sit shyly,* GOLDA *in the chair down left not turning, each in a separate pool of light; they talk looking straight ahead, dreamlike.*) —by letter is no way, Goldie, I'm tired of living with you in a mailbox.

GOLDA. Oh, Morris, I've told you I love you—

MORRIS. I want us to be married now.

GOLDA. —but there's something else now.

MORRIS. Who?

(*The* MOTHER *and a teen-age* CLARA—*the sister— come down right, bearing platters and chairs to set the platform as a table; lights on it.*)

MOTHER. (*Shouts.*) Supper, Moishe! Clara, get your poppa.

CLARA. (*Shouts.*) Poppa! Supper!

GOLDA. (*Remains left.*) Momma, this is Morris Myerson, from Denver. I invited him.

MORRIS. I'm very pleased to meet—

MOTHER. And what does he do for a living?

MORRIS. I'm a sign-painter, I—

MOTHER. Mr. Goodstein owns a real-estate office—

MORRIS. —paint signs—

MOTHER. —but take a bite with us, Meyer.

GOLDA. Mr. Goodstein is an old man.

MOTHER. (*Indignant.*) Old!

GOLDA. In his *thirties,* momma.

(*The* FATHER—*the* 3RD *actor—comes in shaking leaf-lets;* MORRIS *brings his chair; all sit, and will address an empty place as* GOLDA.)

MOTHER. Moishe, this is Meyer Morrison, from Denver.

MORRIS. Myerson.

MOTHER. He wrote the letters.

MORRIS. Schubert when he died left eleven dollars.

FATHER. What?

MORRIS. (*Gently.*) He owned a music office—in his head—

GOLDA. Morris dear, money isn't the thing.

FATHER. (*The leaflets.*) Look, Blume, all over the street by the synagogue—

MOTHER. Eat, everybody—

MOTHER, CLARA. (*Together.*) —it shouldn't get cold.

MORRIS. Goldie, let me not to the marriage of true minds admit impediment.

FATHER. What?

MORRIS. Love is not love which alters when it alteration finds—

GOLDA. What, Morris?

FATHER. (*Baffled.*) Not a word he says!

MORRIS. The sonnets?—they're very high on the list I sent.

GOLDA. Morris, the list was so long—

FATHER. (*The leaflets.*) See, a spectacle she's making of me!

MOTHER. Eat, eat—

MOTHER, CLARA. (*Together.*) —we'll fight later.

FATHER. No daughter of Moishe Mabovitch on a soapbox outside the synagogue is making speeches!

GOLDA. Look, *in* the synagogue they don't let me talk—

FATHER. When you're a man you'll talk *in* the synagogue!—so wait. You hear?

GOLDA. Deaf I'm not, poppa, just female.

FATHER. Good. It's not a nice thing, Goldie, a girl on a box—

GOLDA. I'm talking tonight. On a streetcorner.

FATHER. On a box?

GOLDA. All the comrades are meeting me there.

FATHER. *I'll* meet you!—and drag you home in the street—

GOLDA. Poppa, I promised!

FATHER. —by the braid! You heard it?—tonight you stay home or by the braid! (*He contemplates* MORRIS.) Denver.

MORRIS. Yes.

FATHER. So what are you doing in Milwaukee?

MORRIS. Marrying Goldie. (*The parents stiffen; a silence.*)

GOLDA. The thing is, I don't want to be "Morris's wife"—

MOTHER. (*Relieved.*) Ah—

GOLDA. —and don't want not to be Morris's wife.

FATHER. (*Not relieved.*) Oh?

MORRIS. It's a bissel not clear.

GOLDA. I mean women live so *small*, stuck in the kitchen, and outside the whole world is calling us to come change it—

MORRIS. Goldie child, for thousands of years men have been changing the world, always for the worse.

GOLDA. —how can I just make motza-balls?—in Pinsk this year by the old church Petlura stood the Jews up and shot them—families we knew—

MORRIS. It's very different here.

GOLDA. Here?—we'll disappear.

MORRIS. So perhaps we should, it's nature's way with the superfluous.

GOLDA. And marry you here *I'll* disappear. (*A silence; the parents relax.*)

FATHER. Good. Meyer—

MORRIS. Morris.

FATHER. —the letters we read—

GOLDA. What?

MOTHER. Moishe!

FATHER. —not exactly read—

GOLDA. What letters?

MOTHER. Everybody knows in English I can't read—

GOLDA. What letters?

CLARA. (*Jumps up.*) The letters Morris wrote you—Goldie, I swear I didn't want to—

MORRIS. You read *our* letters?

FATHER. Just yours.

MOTHER. —not read even, Clara told them to me in Yiddish—

CLARA. She made me, Goldie—

MOTHER. What's happening to my daughter I have to know!

CLARA. —but I left out the best parts—

FATHER. The point is—

GOLDA. (*Coldly.*) Clara, it's not what socialists do.

CLARA. Oh, I hate everybody— (*She runs out in tears; the* MOTHER *rises to go after her.*)

MOTHER. Fight, fight—we'll eat later—

FATHER. The point is, we know you from the letters, Meyer, and the answer is no.

GOLDA. The answer is yes!—I'll give the answer—

MOTHER. (*Off.*) Moishe, come out here this minute, you—you—

FATHER. Excuse me.

MOTHER. —naarische kopf!

(*The* FATHER *hurries out;* MORRIS *stands behind* GOLDA.)

MORRIS. So it's yes.

GOLDA. No, it's maybe. Morris, you're a wonderful person, and know everything I don't, but a life so squeezed in?—oh, someday there'll be a world where poor Jews open up like flowers, no meanness, no war, no disease or capitalist inequality—

MORRIS. (*Dry.*) Someday. Meanwhile?

GOLDA. I want a part in building it. The women there are ploughing the land, sharing with the men the dangers and hard work—

(*The* MOTHER *and* CLARA *return, to clear off, but leaving the chairs.*)

MORRIS. Women where?

GOLDA. —Rachel Bluwstein, Rachel Yanait—

MORRIS. Who?

GOLDA. —in Palestine, pioneers. New women, wives and mothers they are also—

MORRIS. Palestine.

GOLDA. —but not just.

MORRIS. You want to go to Palestine—

GOLDA. A parlor Zionist I don't—

MORRIS. —not marry me?

GOLDA. I want to marry you *and* go to Palestine.

MORRIS. Goldie, I like the city, concerts, libraries, I don't like rocks and Arabs. Here I can find work, a little flat—and a quiet wedding, a judge, no chuppah, not religious, just—

MOTHER. (*Turns.*) No chuppah!

MORRIS. Mrs. Mabovitch, you see we're—

MOTHER. I'll kill myself, no chuppah—

GOLDA. Momma.

MOTHER. —in a dogcatcher's office you'll get married?—

MORRIS. —very enlightened socialists, but—

MOTHER. —the Rebbeh will spit me in the face—

MORRIS. —if a chuppah is so important—

MOTHER. I'll leave the city!

GOLDA. Momma, there maybe won't be a wedding!

MOTHER. (*Wildly.*) Why are you doing this to me? (*She marches out,* CLARA *following;* MORRIS *is alone with* GOLDA.)

MORRIS. Goldie, dear revolutionary, if your poppa won't allow you out to the streetcorner?— Palestine isn't so near—

GOLDA. I'm going tonight to the streetcorner.

MORRIS. At seventeen, don't—make up your mind—

GOLDA. And to Palestine whenever. (MORRIS *stands, unhappy.*)

MORRIS. Goldie child, I don't want to plough the land. The spirit I—envy, but human beings suffer, if they suffer in Jerusalem instead of Pinsk is that better? (*A pause.*) I'm—not the happiest person alive— (*He turns out, the lights dimming on him; sound rises—one air-raid siren wailing—and lights up on* GOLDA's *lamp-lit office and the* 2ND *actor in army windbreaker; she trudges up.*)

2ND. (*Drawing.*) It's not hopeless, Golda. You want the details?

GOLDA. Of course.

2ND. We held on. by our eyelids today— (*He marks the desk-map.*) —they took Nafekh, we took it back; they got as far as Snobar here—

GOLDA. Ach.

2ND. —five minutes from the Jordan. Now, can we knock them off balance?—the reserves are up, Musa's 14th on the El Al road, Laner with four bridges here at Yehudia and Aleika. If we counterattack—in a pincers, so—

GOLDA. When?

2ND. In the morning. It's dangerous, a one-to-three ratio we accept, we're fighting one-to-five; we need Dado's consent—

GOLDA. Dado called an hour ago.

2ND. Oh?

GOLDA. He's counterattacking on the Suez.

2ND. When?

GOLDA. In the morning. We're fighting on three fronts—

2ND. Three?

GOLDA. Egypt, Syria, and time. Eban expects at the UN a Soviet move for a cease-fire, to freeze the lines.

2ND. So they start nearer, next time?

GOLDA. I said no. Chaim, will you come back to the army, take a command again?

2ND. If it's a real command.

GOLDA. Dado will consent. Do you pray?

2ND. Do you?

GOLDA. I'll try anything. (*She gathers up folders from the desk*—) Nu, Goldele, so clever— (—*and puts out the lamp; they begin to descend.*) My mother Blume would prove God exists—

2ND. How?

GOLDA. —why else does it rain?—so from a school-book I explained meteorology; she said, Nu, Goldele, if you're so clever you make it rain.

2ND. Rain won't help.

GOLDA. What will?

2ND. Killing them.

GOLDA. (*Long pause.*) In heaven I'll—maybe—for-give them for killing our boys; one thing I'll never forgive—

2ND. What?

GOLDA. —making us kill theirs. (*She dumps the folders on the chair, moves it up center as lights die, and sits; the 2ND actor leaves, and up right the 3RD brings another chair down center, places it reversed, and comes down front as the 4TH Witness, a different role.*)

4TH WITNESS. Golda?—Rachel weeping for her chil-dren, and if you're in her way get off the earth. I sat on a UJA committee with her in New York, debating all day do we add an extra twenty-five million or fifty to the drive, earmarked for Israel, what's realistic?—we voted twenty-five, secret ballot, by one vote. Done with?—no. Golda said, I want to know how every-body voted. So man by man she went around the table, how did you vote? how did you vote? and a sweetheart I'll call Harvey, who's devoted his life to Israel, was the one she picked; she slid him a note. He read it, and went white. Golda walked out. I ran after to stop her at the elevator, she broke away, said, No, no, it's your fault, you're no good, and rode down. I went back, and the note was shaking in Harvey's hands, it said, Your vote is a vote for the Arabs. (*In the dark behind him the other actors—the* 4TH *in army khaki—come in separately with folders to move the supper chairs.*) He's been carrying that note in his wallet for years, waiting for her to take it back. (*He turns to join the others; sound explodes—a huge cacophony of war, all out—while the five actors seat themselves downstage from* GOLDA *as around a circular table in cabinet meeting. Lights up, sound dies, the talk becoming audible—the* 5TH *actor, in a different role.*)

5TH. (*With a folder.*) —and figure the cost at ten billion pounds. So, first a compulsory war loan of one billion. On income, a sliding tax, from 7 per cent up to 12—you have the figures—interest at 3 per cent, refunded in fifteen years. Second, a voluntary war loan of another billion, the response is already tremendous. And third, abroad. I leave this week for fund-raising, Europe and the States. (*He closes the folder;* GOLDA *looks around.*)

GOLDA. Anybody?—so, the front lines. Moshe?

1ST. The chief of staff— (*The* 4TH *actor rises sombrely, stands a map on the reversed chair, and talks from it.*)

4TH. First priority, the Golan news is better. Very heavy fighting, but from Juhader we're closing this pincers; if we can clean out the Hushniyah pocket tomorrow we'll push them back to the UN line, but it's no rout. Yesterday on the Suez—

1ST. Everything went wrong.

4TH. —we ran into a stone wall. Worse, orders got confused, the attack developed not down their north flank—

5TH. Orders got confused?

4TH. War gets confused, yes—

2ND. What happened?

4TH. We went straight into the teeth of the bridge-head—antitank missiles, thousands of infantry, Katy-usha rockets, artillery—an inferno. We sent tanks in like cavalry without air support—we couldn't get through the missiles—and they took heavy losses. And we lost a number of positions here in the Hamutal area. It was a very bad day, we can't afford another one like it. (*A silence.*)

GOLDA. (*Low.*) You have casualty figures?

4TH. Not yet. High, high.

GOLDA. (*Pause.*) You plan what?

4TH. Hold, and let them have losses attacking us. On the positive side, here we found the boundary between their Second and Third armies, and it's soft. That's all. (*He sits; the* 1ST *rises.*)

1ST. Two points. First, the Suez command is fighting among itself—

GOLDA. What?

4TH. Gonen's asked me to relieve Sharon.

GOLDA. No. Sharon?—

4TH. A sonofabitch to get on with, but—

GOLDA. —what a fighter—

1ST. We need a new commander down there—

4TH. Agreed.

1ST. —and our choice is Bar-Lev. Second, the war itself. Materiel is being squandered on counterattacks, and no help from the Americans to make up our losses—

GOLDA. Some items in the pipeline we'll get, Dinitz says Kissinger is sympathetic, but—

1ST. Then what's the delay?

GOLDA. Kissinger has other interests besides us. What's he thinking?—detente, don't offend Brezhnev,

oil, Faisal is talking embargo, Watergate, the White
House is already shaky, Vietnam, another one they
can't have—

1ST. Some units are fighting with their last shells.

GOLDA. —so I have to see a way.

1ST. In three days we've lost 10 per cent of the **air**
force, how many hundreds of tanks?—we can't **throw**
them back now. We *can* retreat to new lines they can't
cross. (*He waits.*) Yes or no?

4TH. That's what you'll say on TV tonight?

1ST. It's the truth.

GOLDA. You're on TV tonight?

1ST. Yes. (*A silence;* GOLDA *rises heavily.*)

GOLDA. Sunday is Ben-Gurion's birthday, we'll send
him a greeting?

3RD. I'll draft it— (*The meeting breaks up, some
leaving with chairs, some standing in gloomy con-
versation; the* 1ST *catches* GOLDA *downstage.*)

1ST. Golda, I'd like an answer.

GOLDA. Do me a favor.

1ST. Of course.

GOLDA. Don't go on TV tonight.

1ST. Why?

GOLDA. You'll be terrible for morale.

1ST. The country has a right to the truth.

GOLDA. Stay home tonight or by the braids.

1ST. What?

GOLDA. Nothing, an old head's full of things, I'll
send Yariv instead.

1ST. Is that your answer? (GOLDA *stands with eyes
closed; light fades on the others, as they leave, and
changes to memory*—)

GOLDA. (*Slowly.*) Stones—

1ST. (*Receding.*) What?

GOLDA. (*Into herself.*) —in 1948 our answer was
stones— In the Etzion ambush our boys were found
dead with stones in their hands. And Ben-Gurion
said—

(—*while backlighting silhouettes on the platform up
right a man on a chair, the* 1ST *Witness as* BEN-
GURION, *half averted.*)

BEN-GURION. Is Kaplan right?—he's just back.

GOLDA. (*Not turning.*) What does he say?

BEN-GURION. Not more than six million from American Jews, don't count on it.

GOLDA. Why?

BEN-GURION. They're sick of us. Goldie, I wake up
in a sweat, what's going to happen to us?—the British
leave, the Arabs will attack, we have nothing.

GOLDA. The Haganah is nothing?

BEN-GURION. Do you know what the Haganah has
cached away?—

GOLDA. Not to the—

BEN-GURION. —ten thousand rifles, not two thousand Sten guns. Sixty mortars, they make a noise.
Against five armies?— I don't sleep, what's going to
happen to us? (GOLDA *drops her folders on the bed-
platform down right, picks up from it a handbag.*)

GOLDA. (*Slowly.*) I haven't been there in ten years—

BEN-GURION. (*To himself.*) Tanks I can get in
Czechoslovakia for ten million—ammunition another
ten—

GOLDA. —but I speak a good American.

BEN-GURION. I must go, yes.

GOLDA. Where?

BEN-GURION. To the Jews of the States.

GOLDA. Leave here now? Look, what you can do
here I can't; there—?

BEN-GURION. I must go myself.

GOLDA. B. G., it's out of the question.

BEN-GURION. (*Suddenly.*) All right. Go today.

GOLDA. My coat's in Jerusalem—

BEN-GURION. Don't even go back to Jerusalem. (*The lights lose* BEN-GURION, *unmoving, and* GOLDA *comes center with her handbag to face us; a* GIRL *from left meets her with a cloth coat, drapes it over her shoulders.*)

GIRL. Welcome to America, Mrs. Myerson.

GOLDA. Thank you, Fanny, where's my sister?

(CLARA—*middle-aged,* LOU *in a different role—hurries in from right.*)

CLARA. Goldie, Goldie!

GOLDA. Clara. (*They embrace.*) Clara, I must talk with Henry Montor.

CLARA. He's in Chicago.

GOLDA. What's in Chicago?

CLARA. The Council of Jewish Federations, they're meeting day after tomorrow—Goldie, you should talk there!

GOLDA. Could I?

GIRL. It's not Zionist, Mrs. Myerson.

GOLDA. Call him. See.

GIRL. It's for the communities here, welfare, new hospitals, temples—

GOLDA. It's *all* the Jews.

CLARA. Yes, pro, anti—

GOLDA. Call him.

(CLARA *and the* GIRL *leave;* GOLDA *remains facing us; a* CHAIRMAN *steps in, right.*)

CHAIRMAN. Friends. We have with us today an unexpected visitor from Palestine, who has asked time for a few words. She is currently on the executive of the Jewish Agency there, Mrs. Goldie Myerson. (*He leaves;* GOLDA *stands center with the handbag, in the coat. Lights fade to around* GOLDA.)

GOLDA. I have no speech. I'll tell you what's in my heart. Fifty-four days ago the UN voted to partition Palestine—an Arab state, a Jewish state—thirty-three nations for, thirteen against. It wasn't the real vote. Six million corpses crying out in the graveyard of Europe cast the real vote. That night I spoke from the balcony of my office in Jerusalem, to hundreds of Jews hugging, singing, dancing; I talked to the Arabs. "The plan is a compromise, not what you wanted, not what we wanted. But now let's live in friendship together." On another balcony an Arab lady said to a newspaperman from America, "Let them dance, they'll all soon be dead anyhow." Next day seven Jews were killed in an Arab ambush on a bus. Two days later an Arab crowd set the Jewish center of Jerusalem on fire. Not a week goes by without a horror. I didn't come to the States only to save seven hundred thousand Jews after we've lost six million. But if the seven hundred thousand in Palestine can keep alive, then the Jewish people as such is alive. If they're killed off too, we're through with the dream of a Jewish people. In May the British pull out, and five nations wait to massacre us. If we have arms to fight with, we'll fight with them. If not, we'll fight with stones. The question is what can we get immediately— I don't mean two months from now, I don't mean next month. I mean now. I've come to tell you that within a very short period, a couple of weeks, we must have in cash twenty-five million dollars. We've never told American Jews what to do. But you have two choices; we have only one. You cannot decide

whether we should fight or not. We will. That decision
is taken. Nobody can change it. You can decide only
one thing, whether we will live. And I beg of you—
don't be bitterly sorry three months from now for
what you failed to do today. (*Silence.* GOLDA *stands,
while the* GIRL *comes to take the coat, leaves; lights
silhouette* BEN-GURION *on his platform.*)

BEN-GURION. (*Rises.*) Fifty million dollars—

GOLDA. For guns.

BEN-GURION. Goldie, when history is written, it will
say there was a Jewish woman got the money that
made the state possible.

GOLDA. For guns. Change the world— (BEN-GURION
goes off.) —it changes you; something—wicked's in
things; that's the dybbuk. (*She goes to the bed-plat-
form, sits, picks up her phone—*) Dinitz. . . . (*—and
lights a cigarette. Up right the* 5TH *Witness—the* 1ST
*actor, a different role—comes to the chair on the plat-
form.*)

5TH WITNESS. Golda, of course, I sit across from her
in the Knesset; she's a fossil. I'm not one of her ad-
mirers. I don't mean the hypocrisy—as Foreign Minister she broke men for sleeping around, if *she* slept
with someone it was for the cause—but this war was
predictable. Jews are standing with guns over an oc-
cupied people, why?—

GOLDA. . . . No, tell him call me as soon as he's
back, I want to come see Nixon myself, incognito.
(*She hangs up.*)

5TH WITNESS. —because the Lady hasn't changed
since she was thirteen, it's them or us, the world is
rotten and hates Jews, she's so calcified there's a joke,
she won't take yes for an answer.

GOLDA. (*To herself.*) Still for guns. Tell me— (*She
stubs out the cigarette, looks skyward—*) —my friend,

in the grain of this world you made, so deep a twist of evil, in all of us. What for? (*—waits—*) Top secret. (*—and lies down heavily with a blanket, in her clothes; the dying lights focus on her. The* 5TH *Witness takes up the chair—*)

5TH WITNESS. Doubts?—she sleeps like a rock. (*—and goes off. The lights on* GOLDA *dreaming linger, still linger; and then on the platform above her they find the* SMALL GIRL *again as before, sound steals in around her—hoof-beats, rising into shouts, windows smashing, a pogrom—and the girl stands screaming; until the lights lose* GOLDA, *and the girl too.*)

ACT TWO

The actors seat themselves on the chairs at rear; house lights off; the dialogue begins in the dark.

GOLDA. Simcha—

5TH. —no, I've discussed it with him, and I think it's the last thing they want.

GOLDA. Why?

5TH. It embarrasses them; a visit by you in war-time— (*Lights pick them out as they come downstage to take up their phones, the 5TH actor sitting to his down right, GOLDA at her desk with a cigarette.*) —will identify them with us so openly it's a provocation—

GOLDA. Incognito, who'll know?

5TH. —to the Soviet Union. Kissinger says how can we keep you incognito?—

GOLDA. (*Bitterly.*) I'll wear my Arab outfit.

5TH. —and a visit's not necessary because the President already approves in principle all our requests.

GOLDA. What's that mean, in principle?

5TH. It means whenever the Pentagon can charter civilian planes to—

GOLDA. Ich ver meshugah duh, *where are the things?*

5TH. Golda, you have no idea the red tape I'm—

GOLDA. Boys are dying here! Call Kissinger back.

5TH. I can't call anybody now, it's three o'clock in the morning here.

GOLDA. Wake him up, does he know the Soviets are airlifting to Damascus?—

5TH. Yes.

GOLDA. —where are they chartering planes, Eskimos—

47

5TH. Golda, all I do is run between the White House and State Department and this Embassy, I'm sleeping here, I haven't been—

GOLDA. (*Harsh.*) Everybody's sleeping there!

5TH. I can't call anybody till dawn.

GOLDA. All right. All right. Let's go back to '56—

5TH. '56.

GOLDA. —I was four months at the UN fighting off Eisenhower and Dulles, we went to a senator named Lyndon Johnson—

5TH. He's dead.

GOLDA. —who wrote a letter in the *New York Times*.

5TH. (*Pause.*) Ah.

GOLDA. The White House is walking five tightropes, a big tsimmis it can't have—

5TH. You want me to go public?—in the press?

GOLDA. I want you to say we'll go public.

5TH. There's a difference between saying and—

GOLDA. Of course, of course, we'll save the difference, what time is it?

5TH. Three o'clock.

GOLDA. Sleep till seven. (*She hangs up, busies herself over papers; the* 5TH *actor leaves as the* 3RD *in khaki comes in to* GOLDA's *office with letters.*)

3RD. This I think you should see.

GOLDA. (*Not looking up.*) They're waiting downstairs.

3RD. From a mother in a kibbutz—

GOLDA. I can't now.

3RD. —with two sons, both killed Saturday. (GOLDA *raises her head; the* 3RD *proffers the letter.*) In the Golan.

GOLDA. Read it.

3RD. Just the end. ". . . happy boys and wanted very much to live and didn't hear what their general said yesterday, You have saved the people of Israel. Mommele Golda, don't cry for us. Be brave."

GOLDA. (*Pause.*) Leave it.

3RD. You want me to answer?

GOLDA. I'll answer it. (*The* 3RD *goes out;* GOLDA *puts on glasses, reads, while from up right a woman comes to place a chair at center—another Witness,* SARILE *from the garden scene.*)

SARILE. '56. That October my mother—Golda Meir now, Ben-Gurion had just made her Hebrew— spent a weekend I won't forget in Revivim. It's the kibbutz my husband and I helped start in the Negev in the early '40's, nothing then, not a tree, not a bird, for a year we lived in a cave, and the water we drilled for was salty, we drank it for *ten* years—people say so offhand we made the desert bloom—but in '56 the trees were young; that weekend my mother played with her grandchildren under them. She was Foreign Minister then, with a secret to keep. On Monday war would break out, and the Egyptian Army *could* strike back through our kibbutz; her grandchildren were in its path. She went back to Jerusalem without a word. The war began the next day, and was over in a week; and after when I said, But momma, why didn't you warn me? she said, I couldn't tell everybody, how could I tell one? (*She leaves;* LOU *enters below left to meet a two-man TV team—the* 1ST *Witness and* 2ND *actor, different roles—coming in from right with an ashtray-stand for the chair.*)

LOU. No ashtray.

TV INTERVIEWER. You're joking.

LOU. She doesn't smoke on television.

TV INTERVIEWER. Must be the one place, kill it. You heard the latest?

LOU. (*Cool.*) I think so.

TV INTERVIEWER. No, Golda and Nixon are com-
plimenting each other's foreign ministers, Golda says
but Kissinger is so smart, Nixon says but Eban is so
cultured, Golda says but of course we both have Jews,
Nixon says but yours speak better English— (GOLDA
by now has come down, letter in hand.) Right here,
Mrs. Meir. Five minutes? (GOLDA *nods, sits; the light
floods her.*) I'll stay off-camera, a few questions—

GOLDA. The lights are too hot.

TV INTERVIEWER. I'm sorry, we have to see you, I
promise it's not—

GOLDA. People shouldn't see me sweating, it'll worry
them. Turn them down.

TV INTERVIEWER. You won't sweat; if they can't see
you, sharp and clear—

GOLDA. What's more important?

TV INTERVIEWER. Mrs. Meir, trust me. Ready?
We'll— (GOLDA *gets up, walks away left.*) Cut them
in half! (*The light is cut;* GOLDA *comes back, sits.*)
Better? (GOLDA *nods.*) You have a statement?

GOLDA. I'll make one.

TV INTERVIEWER. Ready?— Go.

GOLDA. (*To the camera.*) I'm able to tell you today
the Golan Heights are back in our hands. I want to
stress not who but what we're fighting against. Thirty
years the British army tried to hold down two thousand years of Jewish hopes; they couldn't. Nobody
will. It's a promise, written in the Torah—and in the
stars—to homeless people, you'll find your way home
again. I mean all people, including our neighbors,
there's no question that can't be settled if they grant
us one right. To exist here. For six years one of the
two strongest nations in the world has been supplying
them with arms—rockets, tanks, planes—the most
sophisticated weapons to kill with, and this all in the

name of socialist ideals. But if human life doesn't
matter, what do you have ideals for? The war isn't
over. When it does end, it will end in victory.

TV INTERVIEWER. Madam Prime Minister, in a
Jordanian communique today there was word of
mobilization there. Will Jordan enter the war?

GOLDA. I don't know. I can say only this, an intelli-
gent leader—once before he was asked not to enter a
war—should have a good memory.

TV INTERVIEWER. You didn't mention the Egyptian
front.

GOLDA. There we are holding, close to the Canal.

TV INTERVIEWER. Will we cross it?

GOLDA. (*Dry.*) We haven't been invited.

TV INTERVIEWER. Can you say at this stage what
our objectives are in this war?

GOLDA. Peace.

TV INTERVIEWER. The Soviet Union is calling for a
cease-fire in place—

GOLDA. But on lines that don't mean they can re-
group for a new attack.

TV INTERVIEWER. It's rumored the United States
also favors—

GOLDA. I can't talk for any other government; we
won't accept a cease-fire in place. If we had word they
were ready to go back to the October 5th lines, we
wouldn't lose many minutes in letting them.

TV INTERVIEWER. A question in the public mind,
what is the price of this war?

GOLDA. Price?—every son who falls. That's a terrible
price.

TV INTERVIEWER. Thank you, Mrs.—

GOLDA. I want to say a word to the mothers. We're
a small country, and one death a whole kibbutz weeps
for; if five boys from Jerusalem die, there's not a

family in the city doesn't know one of them. Jews have always lived close to death, and love life the more; even in our religion there's not a law that can't be broken to save one life. The chosen people never meant to me God chose us, it meant we chose him. It put us at the dangerpoint of everything human. Who knows more about suffering and love and exile and trying—we didn't always succeed—to live by the word we gave the world? Israel was never just a country, it's a—human frontier, and that's what we've given our lives to. And sometimes for.

TV INTERVIEWER. (*Waits.*) Thank you— (*The light is killed.*) —Golda.

GOLDA. Next time listen.

TV INTERVIEWER. I did. Thank you. (*The TV pair leave, right;* LOU *comes from the rear, as* GOLDA *lights a cigarette.*)

LOU. At eleven, the military—

GOLDA. I'll be here.

LOU. (*Brightly.*) —wish to know what to do next.

GOLDA. Win. (LOU *leaves, left;* GOLDA *stands alone, heavy.*) And that's what we've—given our lives to— Morris— (*The lights change to memory,* GOLDA *goes into herself.*) What is the price— (*She waves her thoughts away with the smoke.*) 1928. (MORRIS *in 1928 garb, carrying a package, stands in shadow at rear;* GOLDA *comes front as a Witness.*) 1928 we signed the Declaration of—

MORRIS. '48.

GOLDA. (*Stops.*) '48.

MORRIS. 1928 was your own declaration.

GOLDA. (*A pause, not turning.*) —we signed the Declaration of Independence. Which started, With trust in the Rock of Israel we—and already we couldn't agree, the rabbis demanded we say God and the left wouldn't sign to a rock, and B. G. spent half the day convincing everybody the Rock meant God *or* the people, and Sharef was waiting to rush the scroll to a bank-vault so it would last even if we didn't —from my window I saw four Egyptian Spitfires zoom in to bomb Tel Aviv—and in Washington we couldn't get it to the White House till we agreed even on a name for the state; but then B. G. read out the Declaration to us, very matter-of-fact till he came to, The State of Israel will be open to Jewish immigration and the ingathering of exiles, when his voice broke, and my turn to sign somebody behind me said, Why are you crying so, Goldie?—and in Washington they hurried the paper to the White House without a name, at the sentry-box there was a phone message for the courier, Israel, right there he wrote it in and took it inside. Midnight my phone rang, Goldie, are you listening, Truman has recognized us! —ten minutes after he got it; I always thought under different circumstances he could be Jewish. (*She gathers cigarettes and letter, turns back.*) And that's how after nineteen hundred years of exile we brought the state into being again.

MORRIS. Tell the first story.

GOLDA. What?

MORRIS. 1928. Politics you always—found a hiding place—

(GOLDA *walks away left, in a blind circle, as the* SMALL GIRL *and* BOY *come in night-clothes to stand on either side of* MORRIS; *sound begins, a scratchy record of Caruso singing, while* MORRIS *comes with the package and sits in the chair to unwrap it;* GOLDA *in the shadows behind him sees the children gazing.*)

GOLDA. Go to bed and keep warm, Sarile—

MORRIS. Today I was paid in cash, not scrip. So, being so unexpectedly a man of wealth, I bought something for the soul—

GOLDA. Menachem, for the last time, go to bed! (*The children run off squealing, and* MORRIS *unwraps a lovely lampshade;* GOLDA *stares.*)

MORRIS. Lo and behold. You like it?

GOLDA. (*Flat.*) It's beautiful.

MORRIS. (*Pause.*) You don't like it.

GOLDA. It's beautiful, it's beautiful.

MORRIS. No, it's—not beautiful, now. Goldie dear, the kerosene lamp is so ugly—

GOLDA. Turn the record off.

MORRIS. It's Caruso—

GOLDA. I almost killed a man today.

MORRIS. What?— Who?

GOLDA. Turn the record off! (*She herself turns abruptly, stands in the shadows, and sound stops;* MORRIS *sits with the lampshade,* GOLDA *paces in the shadows.*) Morris, I can't live the—way I—

MORRIS. (*Quiet.*) Tell me about the man.

GOLDA. Nobody wants the scrip, you know that, twenty minutes I have to beg the butcher for half a pound of soup bones, bread and margarine yesterday the grocer wouldn't give me on credit, today—they go to bed hungry!—that grobber-jung downstairs was telling the milkman watch out for us he wouldn't get his money, I picked up a stick—shouting at him and *hitting* him, on the—

MORRIS. Really?

GOLDA. —on the head, on the head—

MORRIS. Was he hurt?

GOLDA. Of course he was hurt, if he didn't run so good he'd be down there yet. It's very beautiful, show

it to Sara, she has a sore throat. (*A silence.*) I sound
like my mother. It's not what I came to Palestine for.

Morris. Goldie dear, how much can a bookkeeper
make?—times are very bad here—

Golda. Look, it's not money.

Morris. —in this paradise—

Golda. I was furious to start with, I came back
from the nursery-yard—

Morris. So give it up.

Golda. Morris—

Morris. I didn't suggest you scrub the whole school's
laundry—

Golda. I can't feed them, I'll *pay* the school? It's
not the work either, I worked harder in the kibbutz—

Morris. Ah!—the blessed kibbutz—

Golda. —and was anyway thinking I should never
have left—

Morris. I was sick!—I—

Golda. —sick of it—

Morris. —didn't ask to dig myself into a grave
either—

Golda. —the worst mistake I made.

Morris. No, you make one before.

Golda. What?

Morris. You married me. (*A silence.*)

Golda. Look. I'm going back to Party work. (*A
silence.*)

Morris. Someone invited you?

Golda. Yes.

Morris. Who?

Golda. I met somebody in Tel Aviv last week, the
Histadrut needs a—

Morris. Who?

Golda. —secretary of the Women's Council; they're
setting up farms to train immigrant girls in—

MORRIS. I thought you stopped seeing those people.

GOLDA. (*Pause.*) I'll find a place in Tel Aviv, there's a—workers' house on Hayarkon—

MORRIS. I work in Jerusalem, Goldie.

GOLDA. —and you can come on weekends.

MORRIS. No. No.

GOLDA. Today I made up my mind.

MORRIS. Go, then. The children stay here.

GOLDA. You'll take them to the office?

MORRIS. You'll take them to the office?

GOLDA. I'll hire help. There's a school.

MORRIS. (*Dazed.*) You—have it all calculated out. Money, work, politics—but it's them—

GOLDA. (*Now the lioness.*) No, I've had enough!—

MORRIS. —all your Party cronies—

GOLDA. —so jealous of my work and friends—

MORRIS. —they steal you from me—

GOLDA. —four years I've given to two rooms here, the worst time of my life, I'm thirty years old, what's my head full of?—bills I can't pay, shoes are falling apart, Sara has a cough, my whole life is bargaining over two chicken-legs—I'm in Milwaukee!—other people like me for the things you hate, I have a mind of my own!—and what I came here for I won't live without.

MORRIS. (*Shaky.*) I followed you from Denver to this wasteland and you'll make me live alone here?

GOLDA. I get smaller ever year.

MORRIS. You're—letting me down, Goldie—

GOLDA. (*Fierce.*) Who let who down?

MORRIS. (*Pause.*) Yes. (*He crushes the lampshade between his hands; GOLDA is stricken.*)

GOLDA. Oh, Morris— (*She comes to the chair behind him; he shifts away from her touch.*)

MORRIS. (*In tears.*) I warned you, I wrote once

didn't you ever think your Morris might lack the—
indomitable will—Loving you is, you're a—thirty-
year-old rock of Gibraltar— (*He gets up, stands a
moment—*) I'll throw this out. (*—and takes it toward
the shadows;* GOLDA *is bent over the chair.*)

GOLDA. Morris, if I'm happier maybe it'll be better
for everybody. I'll try harder, be a good wife, have
the life *I* need—

MORRIS. We'll find out, I'll— Two things I know,
Goldie— (*He comes back, picks up the wrapping.*)
—you won't meet a man who doesn't let you down,
from your poppa with the boards on; the other— (*He
is on his way out, stops.*) I love you for those things
too. I'll never not love you. (*He goes out;* GOLDA
stands alone over the chair, older.)

GOLDA. (*Slowly.*) What is the price?

(*Sound erupts—war, explosions and gunfire—as the
3RD and 4TH ACTORS in khaki come in to her at
left.*)

4TH. Golda, it's a political decision, you have to
make it. (GOLDA *straightens, chain-lights a cigarette.*)

GOLDA. What?

3RD. We've pushed the Syrians off the Heights; do
we push on?

4TH. Eytan can attack tomorrow at eleven with the
7th Brigade; Laner at one on the Damascus road—

GOLDA. What's political?

4TH. Invading Syria. (*Pause.*)

3RD. There's a chance of Soviet intervention.

GOLDA. Yesterday in the Golan—

4TH. It was our best day, yes.

GOLDA. —we lost more boys than any day so far;
you say best?

4TH. Tactically.

GOLDA. Tactically.

4TH. We can't turn to the Egyptians till we break the Syrian army; if we don't break it they'll absorb the Soviet stuff coming in. And we don't have the tanks you promised—

GOLDA. I talk to Dinitz in his sleep. Send the young to die, it's the—

4TH. You know Ran?—17th Brigade—

GOLDA. —the cruelest thing I have to do—

4TH. Wounded Sunday. His brother's in the hospital, another brother was killed with the Barak, I know the parents. I relieved him of his command. (GOLDA *nods*.) He refused to obey, said nobody makes my decisions for me, he's back fighting all bandaged up.

GOLDA. (*Pause.*) But if I can't do it, get out and let somebody do it who can. —You have a complex about the Soviets—

3RD. Perhaps.

GOLDA. Perhaps. So. Let's push into Syria. (*She turns left; the men leave up right.*)

3RD. God help us if she's wrong. (GOLDA *hears, hesitates and trudges up to her office, where* LOU *is gathering dirty dishes from the desk.*)

GOLDA. Leave them.

LOU. No, you hate a sloppy desk.

GOLDA. I'll wash them later.

LOU. My dear Prime Minister, there's a girl.

GOLDA. (*Sits.*) They're my dishes. If this war ever ends, every dish in my house I'll wash again. I miss it.

LOU. Yes, it is an interesting hobby.

GOLDA. If it ends. (*She sits forward, face in hands.*) Why did we take this job?

LOU. You said you would not accept without me.

GOLDA. You could have refused; we'd both be home with our dishes.

Lou. I did.

Golda. I meant to leave after three months—

Lou. Well, you came to like it; and so did I.

Golda. I don't like it.

Lou. There is the power, dear lady.

Golda. Power. Wash a dish it's clean, that's power. (*Lou goes out with the dirty dishes.*) God help us if I'm wrong. (*She is moveless a moment, then paws among papers. From right the* 6TH WITNESS—*the* 2ND ACTOR, *a different role—comes to the chair.*)

6TH WITNESS. Golda?—I've been in the opposition for thirty years, she was nothing but a tough Party workhorse and never popular. Ran for mayor of Tel Aviv in '55 and couldn't get elected; retired in '66, too sick to work, and got 3 percent of the vote in a popularity poll; was made Prime Minister in '69 only as a stopgap—wasn't too sick, somebody said she suffers from psychosomatic health. Like Pavlov, say the word duty and the workhorse salivates. (*He lights a small flame in the floor at center, rises.*) She was always contentious. In London she walked out on Weizmann because he said she was irresponsible; for years she didn't talk to Ben-Gurion because he said she was corrupt.

Golda. (*Not looking up.*) Stupid and corrupt.

6TH WITNESS. And now she's Mother Israel. I'll give you Golda the politico in a nutshell: you're in a dark hall and at the end she's sitting in a light, the earth mother, sending out waves of protective warmth, and you can't resist, you throw yourself on her bosom and the next minute you're dead. (*He takes the chair out right.*)

Golda. (*Waits.*) The last time someone threw himself on my bosom I'm too old to remember; they didn't act dead. (*She rises, as* Lou *comes back with papers.*) I want to cable Dinitz. Go public.

Lou. (*Writes.*) Go public.

GOLDA. Saturday.

Lou. Saturday.

GOLDA. Unless.

Lou. Unless—?

GOLDA. That's all. (Lou *goes out;* GOLDA *comes heavily to the front of the desk.*) I'll give you all of us in a nutshell: you're in a dark hall— (*The lights go dark, the small flame burns on the floor.*) —and the light isn't on me, it's our eternal flame to the six million Hitler killed. Yad Vashem. Yad vashem, it's from Isaiah, I will give you a memorial and a name; we're still trying to collect each name. The building's on a hill outside Jerusalem. (*She comes down—*) You walk up the Path of the Just, each tree named for a non-Jew who risked his life to save one of us; above is what looks like a smokestack— (*—walks upstage—*) —the memorial shaft, out of—heaps of ashes?— (*—stands—*) —and a plaque, Now and forever in memory of those who died sanctifying the name of God; further on— (*—and turns down past the flame.*) —is the Hall of Remembrance. Inside it's dark, except for the flame. It takes a minute before you see, on the floor is writing. Twenty-two names. Buchenwald, Treblinka, Babi Yar, Auschwitz, Theresienstadt-Terezin, Dachau, Bergen-Belsen— (*A long moment of silence.*) Nothing else. Israel?—stand here, everything in it makes sense. (*Slowly the lights begin to come back.*) And outside down the steps for a few cents you can buy a very good knish, because life goes on.

(*The lights rise, as five actors come down separately with chairs, eliminate the flame, and seat themselves as around a circular table in cabinet meet-*

ing; they include a RELIGIOUS MINISTER *in skull-cap—the* 1ST *Witness, a different role.*)

2ND. (*In khaki.*) The Suez problem— (*He waits for* GOLDA *to come sit, downstage, her back to us.*)

GOLDA. Talk, talk.

2ND. —is that our strength is speed and maneuver, and we're nailed down in a static war; they're sitting under an umbrella of missiles. The only way to break it up is cross the Canal.

RELIGIOUS MINISTER. You tried on the 8th.

4TH. No. Wait till they come out to attack, smash it, cross then.

GOLDA. Why should they come out?—I'd sit there under my umbrella—

2ND. They'll come out because their Syrian partner is screaming take the pressure off me.

1ST. What about supply routes?

2ND. The one we make.

3RD. One?

2ND. The one we make. We probed on the 8th between their Second and Third armies, and there's a chance to reach the Canal without a heavy battle. (*He passes a photo.*) Golda, this is the bridge.

GOLDA. Bridge?

1ST. The prize bridge.

2ND. The one Sharon will cross the Canal with. Two hundred yards long, it moves on rollers, tanks tow it; when it goes into the water it spans the Canal.

RELIGIOUS MINISTER. You base a crossing like that on a single supply route?

2ND. Give me two. (*A pause.*)

GOLDA. (*Heavily.*) A crossing is very risky.

2ND. Very. But if they come out from under the missiles, it's our chance. (*A pause.*)

1ST. (*Rises.*) We'll see how it goes in the next two days. (*The meeting begins to break up; they remove chairs.*)

GOLDA: I don't have an easy heart for it. (*They stop.*)

4TH. Golda, there's no choice.

GOLDA. Syria, how are our losses?

1ST. We're bleeding out.

2ND. We're exhausted, Golda—fighting for a week against fresh reinforcements, no time to eat, boys fall asleep halfway into a sentence—

3RD. I said to Benni today we're hoping for more planes; he said, God knows if I'll have pilots to fly them. (GOLDA *sits with bowed head; the* 4TH *lingers behind the others leaving.*)

4TH. Golda, we have two options. A crossing to end the war is one.

GOLDA. What's the other?

4TH. Settle for a cease-fire. (*He walks out after the others; only the* RELIGIOUS MINISTER *remains, and comes to* GOLDA *as she rises.*)

RELIGIOUS MINISTER. I was visiting the wounded, Golda, do you know a soldier named— (*He looks at a piece of paper.*) Mordecai Stern?

GOLDA. Mordecai Stern.

RELIGIOUS MINISTER. Modke?

GOLDA. No.

RELIGIOUS MINISTER. (*With a flower.*) He sent you this, he was one of the Cyprus children—

GOLDA. (*Takes it.*) Cyprus.

RELIGIOUS MINISTER. —he gave you some paper flowers there?

GOLDA. (*Pause.*) I still have those flowers. Yes, give him my love. (*The* RELIGIOUS MINISTER *opens his hands, helpless.*)

RELIGIOUS MINISTER. (*Then.*) I'm sorry. (*He goes out, with the chair;* GOLDA *stands alone, and the lights change to memory.*)

GOLDA. Modke. Modke. (*Up right three children—* BOY, SMALL GIRL, YOUNGER BOY—*in refugee rags stand silhouetted on the platform, gazing at* GOLDA; *down left, the lights next find a* BRITISH COMMAN- DANT—*the* 3RD ACTOR, *a different role—waiting with a letter.*) Cyprus—

COMMANDANT. Mrs. Myerson.

GOLDA. —where, after Hitler, the British ran a con- centration camp for Jews—

COMMANDANT. Our White Paper limits immigration into Palestine.

GOLDA. (*Turns.*) —refugees sailing there by the thousands you stop in mid-ocean, and cage up on Cyprus—

COMMANDANT. We let them into Palestine by quota—

GOLDA. The very people you saved are now your prisoners.

COMMANDANT. My government has a hundred mil- lion Arabs to placate, Mrs Myerson; now what do you expect of *me?*

GOLDA. To do what the letter says.

COMMANDANT. You are permitted seven hundred and fifty a month, you may select them.

GOLDA. The babies and orphans we have a list of; if I can—

COMMANDANT. There is no mention of orphans here.

GOLDA. If the Secretary's forgotten what he prom- ised, I haven't; I'll—

COMMANDANT. He has not forgotten, he sent me a telegram, Beware of Mrs. Myerson. She is a formid- able person.

GOLDA. How nice he remembers.

COMMANDANT. I will have you taken to the huts. There is a committee for each camp, and a committee of the committees; a talkative people. I suggest that you meet first with the committee of the committees— (*He leaves, as the children come down—*)

GOLDA. Hello. (—*to circle* GOLDA—) I'm Goldie, what's your name? (—*and mutely retreat up left to wait, gazing; meanwhile from left and right three* DP's *in rags come in—*) I'm Goldie Myerson from the Agency— (—*to nod and sit on the floor around her. Understudies come to fill out each group in turn.*) I've come about the children. We know how many have died here—

1ST DP. (*Level.*) How many?

GOLDA. Forty-eight.

2ND DP. Forty-nine, today.

GOLDA. (*Pause.*) It's the winter that worries us, we think they won't get through it. The doctors tell us there's dysentery in the huts—

2ND DP. There's no water.

GOLDA. —and an epidemic isn't out of the question.

1ST DP. So get us out.

GOLDA. Every last one—on the day we have a state. Tell me, are some of you due to leave?

3RD DP. (*A woman.*) I'm on the next month's quota.

GOLDA. You have children?

3RD DP. It's my one blessing. No.

GOLDA. Then it's you I came to ask. Will you let a child go in your place? (*The Woman stands up; a silence.*)

3RD DP. It's—first in, first out—

GOLDA. The British will waive it, if the detainees do.

3RD DP. I'm nineteen months here, I'm sick myself,

you want me to die here? (*A silence; the* Dp's *stand up, one after another.*)

1st Dp. This committee has no say on it. You'll have to go to each hut.

Golda. I'll begin in the morning. (*The* Dp's *move away, not leaving; the children come down, circling* Golda, *and the* Small Girl *beckons her to follow*—) What's your name? (—*to up right, where other* Dp's *stand waiting; the children retreat.*) Good morning. (*The* Dp's *sit on the platform,* Golda *stands below.*) Insult you I won't; we don't know what you've been through. What camp were you in?

4th Dp. (*Girl.*) Bergen-Belsen. (Golda *is reading her numbered arm, she pulls it behind her*—) No. (—*and begins to sniffle.*)

5th Dp. (*Pause.*) The officers'—whore. (*The girl jumps up, turns to leave*—)

Golda. I promise you, in Eretz Israel, everything is new. (—*and the girl stops.*) It begins now.

4th Dp. How?

Golda. Let a child go.

5th Dp. Parents go with them?

Golda. How else?

4th Dp. So people who've waited a year for their quota stay, somebody with a child who came last week leaves?—that's what you're asking—

Golda. It's what I'm asking.

5th Dp. The huts have to vote.

Golda. You'll have a meeting?

4th Dp. Tomorrow.

Golda. Can I talk at it? (*The* Dp's *break up, not leaving; the children come to lead* Golda, *the* Small Girl *taking her hand, down left*—)

Small Girl. Ruthie.

Golda. Thanks, Ruthie. (—*to other* Dp's, *sitting*

down on the floor; the children back away.) Good
evening. You know what I'm—

6TH DP. It's all we've been talking since yesterday.

7TH DP. Maybe we'll disappoint you.

GOLDA. It's what they said in the Agency.

6TH DP. It'll take years to empty this camp.

GOLDA. No. You'll have a meeting?

7TH DP. Yes, tonight. (*The DP's stand, not leaving;
the children come to lead* GOLDA *across down right*—)

BOY. I'm Nahum.

GOLDA. So maybe you'll be a prophet too, they had
courage, they didn't care if they got elected—
(—*where other DP's sit on the platform; the* 8TH, *a
woman, rises.*) Good afternoon—

8TH DP. (*Savage.*) I vote yes, you got my vote, now
go away! (*She thrusts past,* GOLDA *takes her elbow.*)

GOLDA. No, don't talk to me like that without a—

8TH DP. I *killed* my baby. (*She breaks away, dis-
appears among the others;* GOLDA *stares.*)

9TH DP. (*Pause.*) She was hiding in a sewer with a
group, the Nazis were above, the baby started crying— (GOLDA *stops it with a hand.*)

GOLDA. (*Then.*) I know that story.

9TH DP. She smothered it.

1ST DP. (*Crossing.*) There's a mass meeting in the
morning, we'll make a recommendation—

GOLDA. Look, I'm not asking you to stay here forever.

1ST DP. If you want to talk to it— (*He leads her
up right on the platform; all the DP's are below now,
and* GOLDA *speaks to them as she walks.*)

GOLDA. We'll have a state. Someday we'll have a
state. (*She stands above them; they wait, scattered,
listening.*) You came from the DP camps of Germany,
France—You remember in every camp schoolroom

there was a map. Of Palestine. The children learned its
geography, sang its songs, talked of arriving—And
the teachers said, Without this map the children would
lose hope. Fifteen thousand children went into the
death camp at Terezin, one hundred came out. If we
lose the children, we lose the future. No. No. If we
lose the children we lose the children. It's up to you.
(*She comes down among them; they part to let her
pass. The* 1ST DP *takes her down front.*)

1ST DP. We'll vote. You wait outside. (*He leaves
her, and returns to the crowd, motionless with backs
to us.* GOLDA *sits on the ground, to wait; and the children come down with a bouquet of flowers.*)

YOUNGER BOY. Goldie? (GOLDA *turns; he hands her
the flowers, made of scraps of paper. After a moment*
GOLDA *smells them.*)

SMALL GIRL. They're only paper.

GOLDA. Really?

BOY. There's no flowers here.

GOLDA. They're the realest flowers I ever saw.

SMALL GIRL. You could put perfume on them.

YOUNGER BOY. (*Points.*) I made this one.

SMALL GIRL. I made this one and—

BOY. I made these three!

SMALL GIRL. —and this one— (*A pause.*)

GOLDA. I'll always keep them. (*The* 1ST DP *comes
back down to* GOLDA.)

1ST DP. They voted.

GOLDA. How?

1ST DP. Yes.

GOLDA. (*Finally.*) I knew they would. (*She gets up;
the* DP's *walk off, in all directions, and* GOLDA *reaches
to stop the younger boy.*)

YOUNGER BOY. I'm Mordecai Stern. Modke. (*He
turns, and runs out after the others;* GOLDA *is alone.*)

GOLDA. Modke.—Choose life. (*She sets the flowers carefully on the ground, and walks to her desk, to sit. She finds a cigarette and tries to light it, but is trembling so her fingers drop it. She gets it lit and picks up her phone, as the* 5TH ACTOR *comes down right to pick up his.*) Simcha.

5TH. Here.

GOLDA. You're seeing Kissinger tonight.

5TH. Yes, very late.

GOLDA. I have a message from him.

5TH. Yes?

GOLDA. Tell him we—Ask him—See if he can get us a cease-fire.

5TH. What?

GOLDA. In place.

5TH. What!

GOLDA. Try for a cease-fire in place.

5TH. It means we've lost! The cabinet really wants it?

GOLDA. Not yet.

5TH. Golda. What happened?

GOLDA. The resources to continue we don't have. Such losses, men, equipment, if we try to cross the Canal and bog down? The casualties, the casualties—

5TH. Ah.

GOLDA. The casualties are—hard to bear—

5TH. I'll tell Kissinger tonight, it's a gruesome message.

GOLDA. Tell him. It's too hard— (*She puts the phone down.*) —to bear so much death. (*Lights change to memory as the* 5TH ACTOR *leaves; sound begins, solo cello playing the Bach saraband, and* GOLDA *sees up right a small group of mourners,* SARILE *and* MENACHEM *from the garden scene, a Rabbi, one or two others, who come down to the flowers. They conduct a brief ceremony—the Rabbi reads a Hebrew prayer aloud,* MENACHEM *joins him in a responsory—and when it is over, sound dies away. All but the family walk slowly off, up right.*) I was away when it happened—

MENACHEM. Always.

GOLDA. (*Pause.*) What was he doing in my house that day?

SARILE. Sitting there, momma.

MENACHEM. Often, didn't you know?

SARILE. People who came for you would find him, sitting.

GOLDA. Yes. I knew.

MENACHEM. So death found him, sitting there.

SARILE. What did he think, sitting alone like that for hours? (*She stands a moment, turns, walks out up right.*)

GOLDA. What I'm thinking now. (MENACHEM *squats.*)

MENACHEM. Morris Myerson. Born, Velish, 1894; died, Tel Aviv, 1951. Loved music, brought with him from Milwaukee all those breakable old records, Galli-Curci, Caruso, Tetrazzini. Loved language, read the poets, Joyce, Proust. And Freud, loved knowledge; went partners with a friend to buy the Encyclopedia Britannica, the survivor to own the books; always gave me books as a present. Didn't think much of politics, loved the things of the—mind, spirit?—he was a strange kind of bookkeeper. I miss him. (MENACHEM *rises, walks out up right.*)

GOLDA. (*Alone.*) Oh, Morris. The best man I knew, such a price I made *you* pay. We didn't live the life we intended. Yes, we have the state; it doesn't keep people from dying. (*She remains at her desk; down left the* 7TH *Witness—the* 4TH *actor, a different role— comes on, to pick up the flowers.*)

7TH WITNESS. Golda, yes, I was at the UN with her

when she was making the speeches. Eban would write
the first draft, she'd correct it—Maimonides? take out
Maimonides, everybody'll laugh at me—but the best
speech she made there was the day she put the text
down and just talked, to the Arabs. She said, Look,
it's the tenth anniversary of Israel. The only way you
recognize us is in trying to wipe us out. Israel is here.
Our greatest grief is the lack of peace with our neighbors. What's the use of pretending Israel isn't here?—
does hate for us make one child in your country
happier? does it turn one hovel into a house? The
deserts are in need of water, not bombers. Wouldn't
it be better to wipe out poverty, illiteracy, disease?—
can't we build a future for the Middle East together?
They didn't look up. (*He goes off left with the flowers;
down right the* 5TH ACTOR *hurries in, snatches up his
phone.*)

5TH. Golda, Golda, Golda. (*The phone on* GOLDA's
desk rings once, twice—) Golda!—Lou, Lior, anyone—
(—*till* GOLDA *picks it up.*)

GOLDA. Yes.

5TH. Golda. Kissinger surprised me, Don't ask for a
cease-fire now—

GOLDA. What?

5TH. He said, You don't ask for a cease-fire when
your back is to the enemy. (GOLDA *hits her fist on the
desk.*)

GOLDA. *Then let him send us help!*

5TH. It's on the way. (*Silence.*) It's on the way!
They're turning the depots inside out, Europe, here,
they'll replace everything—the C-5's are airborne, a
fleet of them, there'll be fourteen Phantoms there by
Monday— (GOLDA *begins to weep.*) Golda?

GOLDA. Simcha.

5TH. Yes?

GOLDA. Thank you.

5TH. Anytime.

(Sound comes in, a distant jet-roar growing overhead, as GOLDA and the 5TH actor hang up, and the entire stage goes sky-blue while the roar passes overhead—then another, then another; the roar is ear-splitting. During it actors run onstage from all directions, gazing up, mute. When the roar subsides, they go off; the 1ST and 2ND actors in khaki enter down right.)

1ST. Golda!—the Egyptians are moving their armor—

GOLDA. *(Turns.)* To attack.

1ST. —they're out from under their missiles—

2ND. The bridge will be ready.

1ST. It must be in the water tomorrow night—

2ND. We assembled it five days ago.

1ST. —the entire time-table is built on that assumption—

GOLDA. *(Comes down.)* Where is it now?

2ND. At Yukon, ten miles from the Canal.

1ST. Sharon will lead—paratroopers, to knock out missiles in range of the bridge—

2ND. We launch a holding attack at five, secure the corridor, tow the bridge in.

GOLDA. Use good chains. *(The men turn to leave.)* Chaim. I'll get the cabinet together, we'll wait for news—

2ND. I'll phone it in. *(They go out, up right.)*

GOLDA. *(Alone.)* Gamble, with more lives, on one drive to end the war— *(She turns left, lights changing to night; LOU is entering with a tray of coffee.)* I'll do

that. Get the Foreign Ministry, make sure Eban under-
stands he's playing for time.

Lou. He does; I'll check it. (GOLDA *turns down
right, where cabinet ministers—the* 3RD, 4TH *and* 5TH
ACTORS, *in different roles, and the* RELIGIOUS MINIS-
TER—*come down with chairs to the low platform, and
settle down for a waiting session.*)

GOLDA. (*With tray.*) All week I've thought about
my life; I began with the brotherhood of man, and
end up as hostess of a war— (LOU *goes up to the
office phone; and* GOLDA *hands out coffee.*)

1ST MINISTER. How soon will they cross?

GOLDA. Any minute.

2ND MINISTER. What did you wire Nixon?

GOLDA. When we win we'll have you in mind.

RELIGIOUS MINISTER. It's not what I will have in
mind.

3RD MINISTER. Who then?—I know, a higher
official—

RELIGIOUS MINISTER. My boy.

GOLDA. Where is he?

RELIGIOUS MINISTER. In the 7th Battalion—with
Sharon.

GOLDA. Well. He has a brave commander.

RELIGIOUS MINISTER. It's what worries me. (*The
phone down right rings;* GOLDA *crosses to pick it up
and converses inaudibly as sound comes in, gunfire
and three half-intelligible voices on radio crackling—*)

   —*Matt here, Matt here.*

   —*Matt, yes.*

   —*Where the fuck are my boats?*

   —*Boats.*

   —*I was promised sixty inflatable boats this
morning at ten o'clock—*

   —*Just a minute.*

—*I moved out at 4:30, I'm in the goddamnedest traffic jam you ever saw, no boats*—
—*They're coming in from Tasa.*
—*Tasa?*
—*They're at the wrong rendezvous, when will you be in the yard?*
—*Never, it's taken me two hours to go three miles*—
—*They'll be waiting for you in the yard*— (—*till* GOLDA *hangs up.*)

1ST MINISTER. So?

GOLDA. (*Then.*) It looks good. They're widening the corridor, very little resistance. Amnon says they're collapsing.

2ND MINISTER. Oh, marvellous— (*They jump up, hug each other with exclamations—"Finally . . . now uncross your fingers . . . it's time, it's time! . . . I'll sleep tonight. . . ."—but* GOLDA *sits again.*) Did they cross yet?

GOLDA. Not yet. It's been postponed.

3RD MINISTER. Till when?

GOLDA. Two hours.

RELIGIOUS MINISTER. Is anything wrong?

GOLDA. Just the supply route, they're making sure.

3RD MINISTER. Be patient.

RELIGIOUS MINISTER. (*Smiles.*) I'm nervous—

3RD MINISTER. Have faith. (*All quiet down. They sit in different chairs, one reads a newspaper, some stand conversing, all smoke, one or two take more coffee.*)

1ST MINISTER. I'm smoking too much.

2ND MINISTER. It's a national disease.

1ST MINISTER. Why?—I don't even like it.

2ND MINISTER. We feel insecure—

3RD MINISTER. We are insecure. (GOLDA *spies* LOU

returning with a paper bag, gets up to meet her, apart.)

GOLDA. It's all right about Eban?

LOU. He will hold them spellbound for a week. What is transpiring here?

GOLDA. (*Pause.*) The bridge is stuck. (LOU *waits;* GOLDA *goes up to the office, sits. The group settles in different chairs; two men exchange newspapers, one works on a chess problem; LOU collects coffee cups, distributes food.*)

1ST MINISTER. It's terrible waiting like this.

3RD MINISTER. Yes, if there was anything we could do—besides wait—

RELIGIOUS MINISTER. (*Stands.*) There is. I should have, before—

1ST MINISTER. Where are you going? (*The* RELIGIOUS MINISTER *walks out, up right.*)

2ND MINISTER. Downstairs.

3RD MINISTER. To the w.c.

2ND MINISTER. To the synagogue.—Here's a riddle, what's the difference between a w.c. and a synagogue?

3RD MINISTER. I don't know.

2ND MINISTER. Don't come to my synagogue.

3RD MINISTER. (*Stares.*) You're getting very tired.

2ND MINISTER. Yes. (GOLDA *at her desk picks up the phone; sound comes in as she converses, great explosions and many voices on radio crackling—*)

—*The Akavish road is open.*

—*No, it's not, goddamit! They came out of their holes and closed it—*

—*Sir, a section is broken down.*

—*Where are you?*

—*Sharon, Sharon!*

—*I can't evacuate casualties—*

—*7th Battalion.*

—*How long to repair?*
—*Just west of the Chinese Farm*—
—*Sharon here.*
—*Two hours, three hours, we're under artillery fire, sir*—
—*Have you infantry to comb the area?*
—*What've they got behind you?*
—*I have infantry, don't know that it's enough*—
—*Tank, missile, bazooka fire*—
—*Matt here, Matt here*—
—*7th Battalion, I'm down to one-third strength*—
—*Nathan!*
—*We're in the middle of a fucking center here! Trucks, guns, dug-in tanks, radar*—
—*Matt here—Sharon!*
—*Nathan, all my tanks are out.*
—*ambulances, thousands of troops*—
—*I've got six half-tracks cut off, I'm moving in on foot*—
—*Sharon here.*
—*Matt here, I'm in the yard with my boats and tanks, I've got rafts for thirty tanks*—
—*Move out.*
—*I'm under shelling*—
—*Move out, move out!*
—*Everything's on fire, it's all hell burning up*—
(—*but the roar of explosions drown out all the voices;* GOLDA *hangs up, comes down to the group.*)

1ST MINISTER. What's the word, Golda?

GOLDA. Our boys are in trouble.

3RD MINISTER. They weren't collapsing.

GOLDA. No. It's very heavy fighting. Very heavy. (*She sits; abruptly then*—) The worst fighting of the war, they said it was all hell on fire there.

1st Minister. Did they say how many killed?

Golda. (*Harsh.*) They can't stop to count the dead!—hundreds, hundreds, they're fighting for the crossroads behind them—

3rd Minister. Is the bridge across yet?

Golda. Not yet. (*She sits again; the* Religious Minister *returns.*) It's broken down.

2nd Minister. What?

Golda. (*Bitterly.*) It's broken down, they were towing it, they're trying to fix it under artillery fire, the man got a prize for the bridge, it doesn't work.

2nd Minister. Broken down.

Golda. They'll fix it.

1st Minister. How long will it take, did they say?

Golda. Three hours.

Religious Minister. Did you hear any word of the 7th Battalion?

Golda. (*Pause.*) No.

1st Minister. Three hours.

3rd Minister. Be patient. You're not fighting.

1st Minister. I'd go home to sleep, but I won't sleep.

3rd Minister. Be patient.—I'll jump out of my skin— (*A silence.*)

Golda. They're in the fighting, of course.

Religious Minister. Of course.

Golda. That's as much as I know. (*The phone down right rings, she picks it up; the others wait.*) Yes? . . . Yes. . . . Yes. (*She puts the phone down. A silence.*) I'm sorry. You've sat up for nothing—

2nd Minister. They didn't get the bridge over?

Golda. No. Not until tomorrow, maybe later.

3rd Minister. Then there's no surprise.

Golda. No.

1st Minister. Are we winning?—losing?

Golda. Killing and dying. Not clear, nobody

knows, it could be a terrible setback. (*She sits again, lights a cigarette; after a moment the others stir.*)

1ST MINISTER. It's very late— (*They straggle out up right, except the* RELIGIOUS MINISTER, *who does not get up; the* 3RD MINISTER *waits for him.*)

LOU. (*Passing.*) I will be in the office. (GOLDA *nods;* LOU *goes off, up left.*)

3RD MINISTER. Come.

RELIGIOUS MINISTER. It's a suffering world, Golda.

GOLDA. (*Pause.*) Why?

RELIGIOUS MINISTER. (*Opens his hands.*) God's will.

GOLDA. It's a question I asked the Pope; he said man's.

RELIGIOUS MINISTER. Man's?

GOLDA. Man's will, the origin of all evil, you Zionists force your will, the Arabs force theirs, neither is God's will, and suffering comes. What he calls will, I call the dybbuk; and Israel *was* born of Zionist will. So it's my fault, the world.

RELIGIOUS MINISTER. What did you answer?

GOLDA. I said, you remind me of my husband.

3RD MINISTER. Did you really?

GOLDA. No; I thought of it afterwards. And I didn't say that ever since one of our young Rabbis said turn the other cheek the most obedient Christians in the world have been the Jews, and it took us into the gas-chambers— That was God's will?

RELIGIOUS MINISTER. How can I think so?

GOLDA. Yes, we *willed* this state into being, so we could live. Some die, others live.

3RD MINISTER. (*Pause.*) Come. (*He goes out; the* RELIGIOUS MINISTER *stays. Another silence.*)

RELIGIOUS MINISTER. It's not as much as you know. Is it?

GOLDA. What?

RELIGIOUS MINISTER. About my son's battalion. (*He waits; she does not look at him.*) Tell me, tell me, Golda.

GOLDA. I heard nothing about names.

RELIGIOUS MINISTER. Numbers.

GOLDA. The 7th Battalion is down to one-third strength. (*They sit unmoving; and presently the* RELIGIOUS MINISTER *begins to weep, with closed eyes, to himself.*) It was a gamble. Some die, others live, was anything in this world ever changed except by some who die for it? If there's a God—

RELIGIOUS MINISTER. There is.

GOLDA. —then he made the dybbuk too, and the dream, and the dying for it.

RELIGIOUS MINISTER. I know there is.—Dying isn't what it seems, Golda, but it hurts.

GOLDA. No, living hurts. I think now, this state doesn't give security. It gives us something better.

RELIGIOUS MINISTER. What?

GOLDA. Opportunities. To be. To do, to hurt, to gamble, lose or win, and die for something better; maybe that's God's will?—I hope your boy lives. (*The* RELIGIOUS MINISTER *stands, starts out, then comes back behind* GOLDA.)

RELIGIOUS MINISTER. In the wilderness, when the children of Israel fought, Moses all day held up the rod of God in his hand; and Israel prevailed. But his arms grew tired.

GOLDA. Yes.

RELIGIOUS MINISTER. So his brothers held up his arms, and his hands were steady until the going down of the sun.—Good night, Golda. (*He goes out.* GOLDA *sits alone a moment, then tries to lift her arms, like Moses, and cannot. She gets up, and trudges to the steps down left. The phone in the office rings, and* LOU

answers it. GOLDA *climbs the steps;* LOU *waits, holding
the phone out.*)

LOU. Sharon is across.

GOLDA. (*Incredulous.*) How?

LOU. On rafts.

GOLDA. Rafts?

LOU. He didn't wait for the bridge. (GOLDA *stands
on the top step, not moving, then does lift her arms—*)

GOLDA. Opportunities— (*—as the lights rise to daylight at center; and* GOLDA *walks down into it.*) At
this hour, our forces are operating on the west bank of
the Canal. (*There is shouting, and all the actors run
in, jubilant, cheering, hugging each other;* GOLDA
quiets it with a hand.) The tide has turned. I can't
say more, there's still fighting to be done. (*She turns
to us.*) There's still fighting to be done, is that news?
Security, no, in all our lives we've had only a choice
of dangers. And we didn't make a paradise. But—
(*The entire cast is in, standing or sitting, listening;
the small flame burns on the floor.*) —seventy years
ago in Kiev my father nailed up boards against a
pogrom; I can still hear the hammer. And to come in
one lifetime all the way from the sound of that hammer to life in a state of our own, where we can defend
our children, and be free, and take in every brother in
the world who wants to come home—what more can
a Jew ask? Our lives have been blessed, whatever the
price. (SARILE *and* MENACHEM *enter last, down right.*)
Opportunities, opportunities, and you'll want younger
blood. I don't blame you, I want some myself. (*She
turns right to leave, sees* SARILE.)

SARILE. Momma.

GOLDA. (*Pause.*) I didn't do very well by my children.

SARILE. Momma—

MENACHEM. It's all right.

GOLDA. You didn't wish many times you had a different mother?

SARILE. Often, but—never— (MENACHEM *takes* GOLDA's *hand. Down left the* 1ST WITNESS *is on a step.*)

1ST WITNESS. Golda?—no more stories, seventy-five years won't go into two hours—

GOLDA. And the time to say goodbye isn't far off. (*She looks around as the actors start to leave, but turns back to us.*) One word more—the best— (*She says it to the audience, face by face—*) Shalom. Shalom. Shalom. Shalom. Shalom. Shalom— (—*until the lights lose her.*)

PROPERTY LIST

Down Right:
One (1) bed platform:
  with handbag under U. L. corner
    with cigarettes, tissues
Two (2) rectangular black boxes
  one U. S. of bed
  one S. L. of bed
Three (3) small black cubes
  one S. L. of black box U. S. of bed
  one D. S. of black box S. L. of bed
  one S. R. of bed
    on cube: red telephone, ashtray with wet blotter,
      notepad, pencil, matches, back-up cigarettes
    in cube: black telephone

Stage Left:
One (1) desk:
  with two (2) folders with papers, ashtray with wet
    blotter, wooden ruler, two (2) pencils, telephone,
    matches
One (1) desk chair set 24″ from desk
One (1) table S. L. of desk
  with five (5) telephones, back-up cigarettes

Down Left:
One (1) rectangular black box
  with telephone under S. R. side

Off Right:
Small black cube
Golda's black blanket
Arab rug
Book "How The World Is Fed"

Arab costume
Two (2) handguns
Cello-bow
Doll (1930's)
Strap of school books
Socialist Leaflets
Dish towel
Cloth coat
Broom
Tablecloth
Four (4) soup bowls
Large bowl gelfilte fish
Four (4) glasses
Jar of horseradish
Seltzer syphon
Four (4) spoons
Four (4) forks
Two (2) buckets, one with ladle
Two (2) flowers
Two (2) pencils
Box of wood
Ashtray stand
TV step unit
Laviler mike
Light meter
Head set
Small white pad
Fruit bowl
Two (2) brass candle lanterns
Kaddish
Two (2) clipboards
Two (2) kerosene lanterns
Two (2) briefcases
Two (2) maps
Folders, papers

Tipped cigars
Miniature cigars
Cigarettes
Lighters
Matches
Small tray with soup dish, napkin, spoon, lighter

Off Left:
Roll of three (3) maps
Staff crutch
Paper flowers
Doll in black dress
Book "Don Quixote"
Ashtray with wet blotter
Tray with perculator, sugar, cream, five (5) cups,
    spoon
Tray with sliced salami and bread
Cigarettes, matches
Cane
Butt can
Folders and Papers
Lampshade
Four (4) books
Elazar's memo to Golda
Lou's papers, pad, pen
Picture of bridge
Two (2) maps
Machine Gun

Intermission:
Reset folders, pencils, ashtray, telephone on desk
Reset telephone table
Rest desk chair 24″ from desk
Reset telephone on D. R. cube

Strike Army jacket from under bed
Strike black blanket from under bed
Set cape under bed
Set handbag under bed
Set glasses on desk
Set dirty dishes on desk
Set cup of hot water on desk at five (5) min.